Quick and Easy
CROCHET

Quick and Easy
CROCHET

100 Little Crochet Projects to Make

Search Press

First published in 2019

Search Press Limited
Wellwood, North Farm Road,
Tunbridge Wells, Kent TN2 3DR

Previously published in 2016 as *100 Little Crochet Gifts* using
material from the following books in the *Twenty to Make* series
published by Search Press:

Mini Christmas Crochet by Val Pierce, 2011
Crocheted Bears by Val Pierce, 2011
Crocheted Flowers by Jan Ollis, 2012
Crocheted Granny Squares by Val Pierce, 2012
Crocheted Beanies by Frauke Kiedaisch, 2013
Crocheted Purses by Anna Nikipirowicz, 2015
Crocheted Hearts by May Corfield, 2015
Granny Square Flowers by May Corfield, 2015

ISBN: 978-1-78221-803-6

The Publishers and author can accept no responsibility for any
consequences arising from the information, advice or instructions
given in this publication.

Readers are permitted to reproduce any of the items in this book
for their personal use, or for the purposes of selling for charity, free
of charge and without the prior permission of the Publishers. Any
use of the items for commercial purposes is not permitted without
the prior permission of the Publishers.

Suppliers
If you have difficulty in obtaining any of the materials and
equipment mentioned in this book, then please visit the
Search Press website for details of suppliers:
www.searchpress.com

CONTENTS

Poppies & Daisies,
page 46

Sailor Girl Beanie,
page 48

Festive Wreath, page 50

Gazania, page 52

Sweet Angel Bear,
page 54

Heart String, page 56

Lily, page 58

Aria Purse, page 60

Square Dance, page 62

Baker Boy Beanie,
page 64

Glimmering Snowflake,
page 66

Tudor Rose, page 68

Betsy Birthday Bear,
page 70

Earrings and Pendant, page 72

Primrose, page 74

Freya, page 76

Daffodil Square, page 78

Fibre Fun Hat, page 80

Christmas Stocking, page 82

Hibiscus, page 84

Katie Wedding Bear, page 86

Heart Brooch, page 88

Rose, page 90

Tate Purse, page 92

Cake Cappuccino Lace Square, page 94

Pretty in Pink Beanie, page 96

Rudolph the Reindeer,
page 98

Foxgloves, page 102

Andrew Bridegroom
Bear, page 104

Snowflakes, page 106

Narcissus, page 108

Cherry Purse, page 110

Scalloped Circle,
page 112

Hippy Chic Beanie,
page 114

Baby Penguin, page 116

Freesia, page 120

Jeffrey Dancing Bear,
page 122

Lavender Heart,
page 124

Himalayan Poppy,
page 128

Lottie Purse, page 130

Catherine Wheel, page 132

Lady Grey Beanie, page 134

Cool Snowman, page 136

Daisy Chain, page 140

Sparkles the Fairy Bear, page 142

Heart Bookmark, page 144

Sunflower, page 146

Bobbles Purse, page 148

Circle in a Square, page 150

Colour Clash Beanie, page 152

Christmas Cracker, page 154

African Violets, page 156

*Mazzy the Keep-Fit Bear,
page 158*

*Chunky Heart Pillow,
page 160*

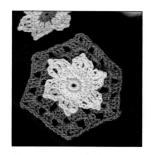

Crocus, page 162

Evie Purse, page 164

Floral Ring, page 166

*Flirty Flowers Hat,
page 168*

Wishing Star, page 170

*Passion Flower,
page 172*

*Belinda Butterfly Bear,
page 174*

Valentine, page 176

Borage, page 178

*Apple Charm Purse,
page 180*

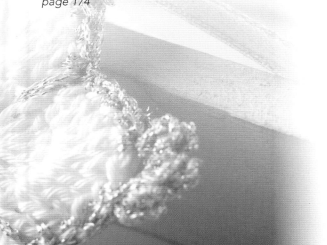

*Circle & Shell Square,
page 182*

*Light and Lacy Hat,
page 184*

Christmas Bell, page 186

Retro Daisy, page 188

*Anthony Garden Bear,
page 190*

Ava Purse, page 192

*Pinwheel Circle,
page 194*

*Making Waves Beanie,
page 196*

*Snowy Fridge Magnet,
page 198*

Carnation, page 200

*Roz the Artist Bear,
page 202*

Myrtle Purse, page 204

*Dog Rose Triangle,
page 206*

*Filet Fun Beanie,
page 208*

Christmas Pudding,
page 210

Scabious, page 212

Bernie the Christmas Elf,
page 214

Lucy Purse, page 216

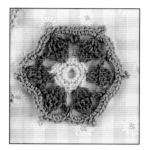

Picot Hexagon,
page 218

Shades of Grey Hat,
page 220

Tabletop Tree, page 222

Orange Blossom,
page 224

Mary Party Bear,
page 226

Isabel Purse, page 228

Autumn Square,
page 230

Street Smart Beanie,
page 232

Poinsettia Gift Topper,
page 236

INTRODUCTION

If you love crochet, *Quick and Easy Crochet* is the perfect book for you. With 100 quick and easy patterns to choose from, there are lots of projects that will appeal to competent beginners and more advanced crocheters alike. Designed by five talented and experienced authors, these fabulous projects are the work of Val Pierce, Jan Ollis, Frauke Kiedaisch, Anna Nikipirowicz and May Corfield.

The range of projects includes beanies, granny squares, flowers, purses, Christmas projects, hearts, bears and granny square flowers, so there is something here for everyone to choose from. There is a handy section on crochet know-how and useful stitches at the beginning, which explains what you need to make these charming projects. Every single one of these beautiful crocheted items will make lovely, personalised gifts for family and friends.

Projects include a Cool Classic Beanie, a Watermelon Purse, a Sweet Angel Bear, a Tudor Rose, a Daffodil Square, a Christmas Stocking, a Lavender Heart and a Sunflower. The techniques used are suitable for crocheters of all skill levels and projects are made in a variety of yarns from lace (2-ply) to super bulky (super chunky) using a wide range of interesting crochet stitches.

Whatever the occasion, there is a wealth of inspiration here with projects that will make the perfect gift for birthdays, christenings, anniversaries, weddings, Valentine's Day and Christmas.

Happy crochet!

CROCHET KNOW-HOW

US and UK crochet terminology

The names for basic crochet stitches differ in the UK and the US. In all patterns, US terms are given first (see Abbreviations on page 19), followed by the UK terms in brackets – for example, US single crochet is written as sc (*UKdc*), and US double crochet as dc (*UKtr*).

Yarn

Most yarns on the market today come ready wound in balls, but some come in hanks which need to be wound into balls beforehand to stop them from knotting. All yarns come in different weights and thicknesses.

A variety of yarns have been used for the projects in this book. They can be substituted, but it is important to check the weight and length of yarn you choose against the ones used in this book to ensure you have enough yarn to finish your projects. Synthetic yarns might be easier to wash, but natural fibres keep their shape a lot better for many years and can be nicer to work with.

Lace yarn (1–3-ply) is a very fine yarn, used mostly for delicate openwork. Some of the projects in this book use the yarn doubled to add thickness (this is noted in the pattern).

Fingering (4-ply) yarn is a superfine yarn, used for most work producing lightweight fabric; fingering (4-ply) mercerised cotton is fantastic for crocheting as it does not split, defines each stitch beautifully and produces a durable fabric with amazing drape.

Light worsted (DK/8-ply) yarn is a medium weight yarn, and is the most commonly used. It can be used for most types of crocheting, from plain, lace and textured, producing medium weight garments.

Worsted/aran yarns (10-ply) are both slightly thicker than DK yarn. Worsted yarn is slightly lighter than aran, but both weights of yarn can be used on projects that call for medium weight yarn.

Bulky (chunky) and super bulky (super chunky) yarns are much thicker and work up quickly and easily for such things as hats, scarves, pillows and blankets.

Gauge (tension)

Many of the projects have been given an approximate completed size, but not a specific gauge (tension). It is not essential to achieve any particular gauge on items that are accessories, so if they turn out a bit bigger or smaller it will not make much difference. However, the finished guide should provide a basic idea of what size your completed project should be if you use yarn of a similar weight. The only projects that have been given a gauge guide throughout are the beanies, and here it is useful to work a gauge sample so that you can be sure that your project will be the size you want.

Crochet hooks

It is essential to work with a hook that is easy on your hands. Crochet hooks are made from aluminium, steel, plastic, bamboo and wood. It is best to experiment with different types to find one that suits you and offers comfort and control.

Other tools and materials

You will need various items such as purse clasps, scraps of fabric for linings, scraps of ribbon, a good pair of scissors for cutting fabric and yarn ends, a tapestry needle for weaving in loose ends and sewing on motifs, and a standard sewing needle and thread.

For some projects it may also be useful to have some iron-on medium-weight interfacing, although this is optional. You will also needs beads, faux pearls, ear wires, jump rings and chain for some of the projects; these items are all listed with the patterns.

Mattress stitch

Mattress stitch is very useful, as it makes a practically invisible and nicely flexible seam for joining pieces of crocheted fabric together.

1 With RS of work facing, insert a tapestry needle through a stitch in the bottom right corner, then across to the bottom left corner, then through both pieces again to secure firmly.

2 Take your needle back to the right edge and insert it a little further up, then across to catch a stitch on the left side.

3 Repeat step 2 to continue.

4 After every few stitches, gently pull the long end of the yarn to draw the stitches together so that the seam yarn disappears and is not visible on the right side of the crochet.

5 Fasten off yarn securely at the other end.

Blocking

The purpose of blocking is to finish off a piece of crochet, make it look regular and professional, and 'set' the stitches. Flat pieces of crochet often benefit from blocking, especially if they are liable to curl at the edges. All you need is a large piece of foam about 1in (2.5cm) thick, a clean towel, a can of spray fabric stiffener (starch), or spray bottle filled with warm water, and some pins.

1 Lay the towel over the piece of foam.

2 Place your piece of crochet in the middle of the towel and spray it with the fabric stiffener or warm water so it is saturated.

3 Now pin out your crochet carefully to the shape you want. You may need to use a ruler if you want a shape of exact dimensions.

4 Leave it to dry, making sure it remains undisturbed.

5 Once it is completely dry, unpin your crochet and it will be a nice, flat regular shape.

Making Pompoms

Pompoms are a great way to decorate all kinds of crocheted projects. To make them, you will need some firm cardboard and some pointed scissors.

Alternatively, you could invest in a set of plastic pompom makers. These are widely available from craft stores and online, and come with full instructions.

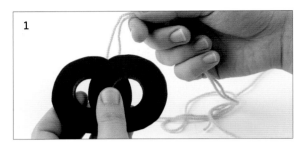

1 Cut out two identical cardboard discs to the diameter of the intended pompom. Mark out a smaller circle in the centre of each disc. This will form a hole to allow yarn to be passed through. As a rule of thumb, this circle should be half the diameter of the outer circle. Cut the inner circles out.

2 Hold the two cardboard discs together and start to wind your chosen yarn round the rings. Cover the ring entirely until the hole in the centre has almost disappeared.

3 With fabric scissors, cut through the yarn between the cardboard discs round the outer edge. Cut round the entire circumference, releasing all of the yarn and revealing the cardboard discs.

4 Tie a spare piece of yarn between the discs to secure the middle of the pompom.

5 Once knotted securely, tear the cardboard to release the pompom.

6 Finish by trimming the pompom into a neat ball.

Crochet Abbreviations

The abbreviations listed below are the most frequently used terms in the book. Any special abbreviations in a crochet pattern are explained on the relevant project page.

US	UK
sl st (slip stitch)	sl st (slip stitch)
ch st (chain stitch)	ch st (chain stitch)
ch sp (chain space)	ch sp (chain space)
sc (single crochet)	dc (double crochet)
hdc (half double crochet)	htr (half treble crochet)
dc (double crochet)	tr (treble crochet)
tr (treble crochet)	dtr (double treble crochet)
dtr (double treble crochet)	trtr (triple treble crochet)
skip	miss
yrh (yarn round hook)	yrh (yarn round hook)
beg (beginning)	beg (beginning)
rep (repeat)	rep (repeat)
sp/s (space(s))	sp/s (space(s))

Crochet stitch symbols

Some of the beanie hats in this book use crochet charts in which you will see the symbols listed below. However, crochet symbols are not universal, so be sure to consult the key that comes with your pattern when using other books.

Key for crochet pattern diagrams

o = 1 ch

• = 1 sl st

× = 1 sc (UKdc)

T = 1 hdc (UKhtr)

 = 1 dc (UKtr)

 = 1 tr (UKdtr)

 = dc2tog, dc3tog or dc4tog (UKtr2tog, tr3tog, tr4tog)

= dc2tog or dc3tog (UKtr2tog, tr3tog)

 = dc4tog or dc6tog (UKtr4tog, tr6tog)

= 3 or 4 dc (UKtr) stitches worked in the same stitch

= 5 or 6 dc (UKtr) stitches worked in the same stitch

 = 2, 3 or 4 incomplete dc (UKtr) stitches worked in the same stitch

 = tr2tog or tr3tog (UKdtr2tog or dtr3tog)

= 3 tr (UKdtr) stitches worked in the same stitch

= 1 dc (UKtr) crochet spike stitch

Tip: If the symbols are joined together at the bottom, then the stitches are crocheted in the same stitch. If the symbols are joined together at the top, then the stitches are drawn through together.

USEFUL STITCHES

Making a chain foundation ring

Foundation rings are useful when you do not need to worry about having a hole in the centre of your work, for example, when making granny squares.

Simply work the number of chains required in the pattern (the stitch on the hook is never counted). Now insert the hook into the first chain you made, wrap the yarn round the hook (yrh) and draw it through both loops to close the ring (that is, make a slip stitch). You can now follow your pattern by crocheting into the ring.

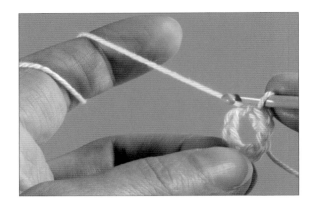

Beginning with two chain stitches

1 First, chain 2. The first round is worked into the second chain from the hook in single crochet (*UK double crochet*). Work the number of stitches required by the pattern (up to 10).

2 There will be a small hole in the centre of the first round. If desired, pull on the starting tail of the yarn to close it up when finishing off. You will need to weave in the loose end securely to prevent the hole from opening up again.

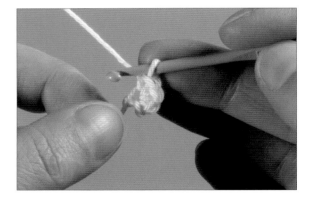

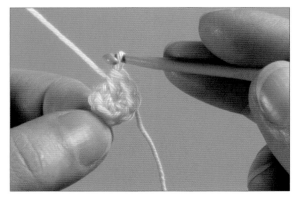

Making an adjustable ring

Instead of beginning with two chain stitches, you can start with an adjustable ring. The advantage of this is that, once the tail end of the yarn is tightened, there is no hole in the centre of your work. This is particularly useful for when you are crocheting toys and other amigurumi projects.

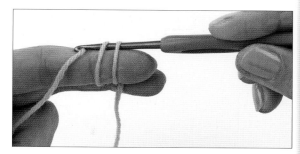

1 Wrap a length of yarn twice around your index finger and slide the hook through the loops.

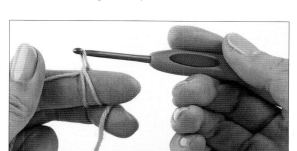

2 Use the hook to pull the end of yarn that is connected to the ball of yarn through the loops.

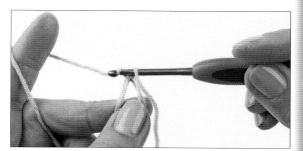

3 Release the ring from your finger, make 1 chain (this does not count as a stitch) and you are ready to follow your pattern, working your stitches into the ring. When you have worked the first round, pull the tail end of the yarn to close the centre hole.

Working in spiral rounds

Working in spiral rounds has the advantage of showing no visible join between rounds and produces an even stitch. It is generally only done when working in single crochet (*UK double crochet*). To work in this way, do not complete each round with a slip stitch into the first stitch of the round but instead continue straight on to the next round. Mark the start of each round by placing a contrasting yarn between the last stitch of the first round and the first stitch of the second round, or by using a stitch holder. Repeat at regular intervals; this will make it easier to count the rounds.

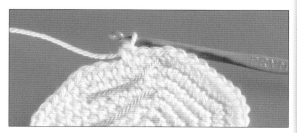

Single crochet two together (sc2tog/UKdc2tog)

This process works two stitches together as one to reduce the stitch count by one. Draw a loop through each of the next two stitches of the previous row/round (three loops on hook), yarn round hook then draw the yarn through all three loops.

Double crochet two together (dc2tog/UKtr2tog)

1 Work a double (UK tr) into the next stitch of the previous row/round up to the point where there are two loops on the hook.

2 Now work into the next stitch of the previous row/round up to the same point so that there are now three loops on the hook. Pass the yarn round the hook and pull through all three loops together.

Changing colour for stripes

1 To change the colour of the yarn for stripes, at the last stitch of the previous row, draw through the yarn in the first colour with a yarn over, so that there are two loops on the hook. Now draw the yarn through these two loops in the new colour. The last single crochet (*UK double crochet*) stitch is therefore worked completely in the old colour and the loop on the hook is now in the new colour.

2 Now crochet one additional turning chain as usual, turn the piece of crochet and continue working double crochet stitches.

Reverse single crochet
(rev sc/*UKrev dc*)

This simply means working single crochet (*UK double crochet*) in the opposite way from normal, i.e. from left to right. It produces a very attractive and decorative cord-like border. Reverse single crochet (*UK reverse double crochet*) is also known as crab stitch.

1 Insert the hook into the last stitch of the previous row/round (the stitch to the right) from front to back. The loop on the hook lies flat on the crochet piece.

2 Draw through the yarn and pull both loops together upwards, so that the stitches are not too tight. Both loops are lying close to one another on the hook. Pull the yarn through both loops.

OLIVIA PURSE

Instructions:

Work beads into each sc (*UKdc*) on second row of colour A; beads are worked on WS of work.

With yarn A and 3.5mm (US E/4, UK 9) crochet hook, make 45 ch.

Row 1 (RS): 2 sc (*UKdc*) in second ch from hook, [1 sc (*UKdc*) in next 4 ch, skip 2 ch, 1 sc (*UKdc*) in next 4 ch, 3 sc (*UKdc*) in next ch] three times, 1 sc (*UKdc*) in next 4 ch, skip 2 ch, 1 sc (*UKdc*) in next 4 ch, 2 sc (*UKdc*) in last ch.

Row 2: 1 ch, 2 sc (*UKdc*) in base of ch, [1 sc (*UKdc*) in next 4 sts, skip 2 sts, 1 sc (*UKdc*) in next 4 sts, 3 sc (*UKdc*) in next st] three times, 1 sc (*UKdc*) in next 4 sts, skip 2 sts, 1 sc (*UKdc*) in next 4 sts, 2 sc (*UKdc*) in last st.

Row 2 forms the pattern.

Work in pattern following the stripe sequence as follows:

Rows 3 and 4: yarn B.

Rows 5 and 6: yarn C.

Rows 7 and 8: yarn D.

Rows 9 and 10 (beaded): yarn A.

Repeat stripe sequence four more times, ending with row 2 of yarn A repeat (beaded).

Making up
Fold work in three parts and secure sides by working a row of sc (*UKdc*) in yarn B, then continue with sc (*UKdc*) along top of inner edge of purse.

Materials:

1 ball each of fingering (4-ply) mercerised cotton yarn in light grey (A), heather (B), rose (C) and garnet (D); 50g/125yd/115m

Hook:

3.5mm (US E/4, UK 9) crochet hook

Notions:

Approx. 144 x small beads

Size:

Approx. 6in (15cm) wide and 3½in (9cm) high

TRADITIONAL GRANNY SQUARE

Materials:

Small amounts of No. 3 crochet cotton in green (A), yellow (B), blue (C) and pink (D); 100g/306yd/280m

Hook:

3mm (US D, UK 10) crochet hook

Size:

3in (7.5cm) diameter

Instructions:

Using A, make 6 ch, join into a circle with a sl st.

Round 1: using A, 3 ch, 2 dc (*UKtr*) into ring, 2 ch, 3 dc (*UKtr*) into ring, 2 ch, 3 dc (*UKtr*) into ring, 2 ch, 3 dc (*UKtr*) into ring, 2 ch, join with a sl st to top of 3 ch at beg of round. Fasten off. You will now have 4 corner sp. Fasten off yarn A.

Round 2: using B, join to any corner with a sl st, 3 ch, 2 dc (*UKtr*), 2 ch, 3 dc (*UKtr*) into same corner sp, *2 ch, 3 dc (*UKtr*), 2 ch, 3 dc (*UKtr*) into next corner sp*, rep from * to * all round ending 2 ch, sl st to top of 3 ch at beg of round. Fasten off. You will now have 4 corner sp and one 2 ch sp between each corner. Fasten off yarn B.

Round 3: using C, join to any corner sp with a sl st, 3 ch, 2 dc (*UKtr*), 2 ch, 3 dc (*UKtr*) into same corner sp, *2 ch, 3 dc (*UKtr*) into next 2 ch sp, 2 ch, 3 dc (*UKtr*), 2 ch, 3 dc (*UKtr*) into next corner sp*, rep from * to * all round ending last rep with 2 ch, 3 dc (*UKtr*) into next 2 ch sp, 2 ch, sl st to top of 3 ch at beg of round. Fasten off. You will now have 4 corner sp, with two 2 ch sp between each corner. Fasten off yarn C.

Round 4: using D, work as for round 3, adding an extra 2-ch sp between the corners and working 3 dc (*UKtr*) into the sp made. Fasten off and work in all the ends.

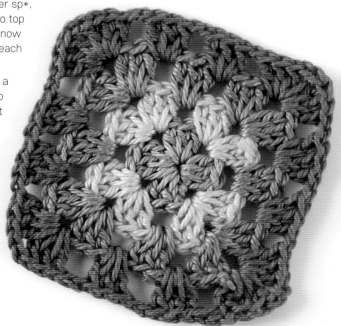

COOL CLASSIC BEANIE

Materials:

2 x balls of aran wool/angora/polyamide blend
   yarn in navy blue; 50g/114yd/105m

Hook:

Size 6mm (US J/10, UK 4) crochet hook

Size:

Head circumference 21¼–23in (54–58cm)

Gauge (tension) sample

12 sts and 6 rounds of dc (*UKtr*) using the 6mm (US J/10, UK 4) crochet hook = 4 x 4in (10 x 10cm). Change your hook if necessary to obtain the correct gauge (tension).

Making a bobble

The band around the beanie has a decorative bobble pattern. Work each bobble as follows:

Bobble: * yrh, insert your hook in the st, yrh and draw through 1 loop * , rep from * to * twice more, yrh, insert your hook in the st, yrh and draw through all 9 loops on the hook.

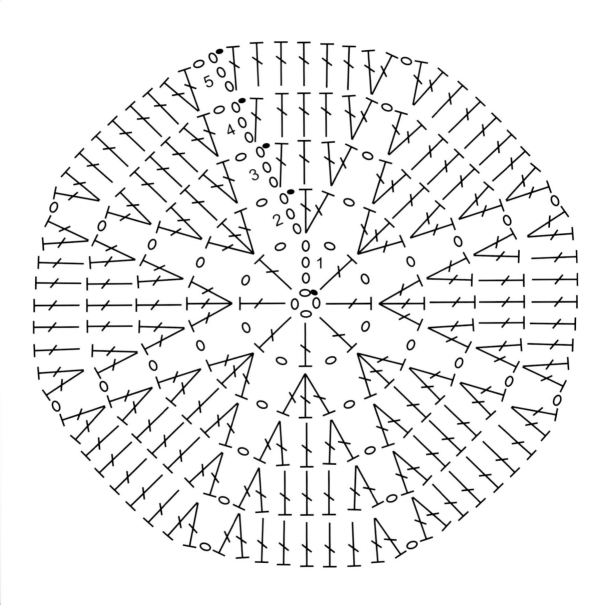

Basic pattern

Work rounds 1–5 following the chart to work dc (*UKtr*) and ch in rounds in the shape of an octagon. Start every round with 1 dc (*UKtr*) (counts as 3 ch) and 1 ch and join up with a sl st into the 3rd ch of the start of the round. Count the 1st 3 ch of the start of the round as the last dc (*UKtr*) of each round. The numbers show the round transitions. The first 5 rounds are shown in full.

Single crochet 2 together (*UKdc2tog*)

See the crochet stitches guide on page 22.

Instructions:

Start the beanie at the crown and work down to the bottom edge in rounds as explained below. This will create the octagonal shape.

Begin with 4 ch and join into a ring with a sl st.

Round 1: Work 3 ch (counts as 1st dc/*UKtr*), then alternate 1 ch, 1 dc (*UKtr*) as shown.

Rounds 2–5: Work following the crochet chart.

Rounds 6–12: Rep round 5, alternating 9 dc (*UKtr*), 1 ch, and working without increases. Make the round transition as for round 5 (80 sts per round).

Round 13: 1 ch then sc2tog (*UKdc2tog*) to end of round; join with a sl st (40 sts).

Round 14: 1 ch then sc (*UKdc*) into every st around; join with a sl st (40 sts).

Round 15: 1 ch, work ∗ 1 sc (*UKdc*), 1 bobble ∗ , rep from ∗ to ∗ to end of round, join with a sl st.

Round 16: Rep round 14.

Fasten off and weave in all loose ends.

PINE CONES

Materials:

- 1 ball of metallic gold light worsted (DK/8-ply) yarn
- Holly berry embellishment
- 20in (0.5m) of narrow gold ribbon
- Toy stuffing
- Craft glue
- Gold thread (optional)

Tools:

Size 2mm (US B/1, UK 14) crochet hook

Sewing needle

Size:

Approx. 2in (5cm) high

Special abbreviations

3dc (*UKtr*) cluster – draw up a loop, yrh, hook into space, draw up a loop, repeat three times, yrh, draw through all loops, 1 ch to secure.

4dc (*UKtr*) cluster – as above but repeat four times.

Instructions:

Using gold metallic yarn, make 6 ch then join with sl st into a ring.

Round 1: work 12 sc (*UKdc*) into the ring then join with a sl st.

Round 2: work a 3dc (*UKtr*) cluster into each sc (*UKdc*), join with a sl st to top of first 3dc (*UKtr*) cluster [12 x 3dc (*UKtr*) clusters].

Round 3: sl st into first space between clusters, work 3dc (UKtr) cluster, 1 ch into each space, join with a sl st to top of first 3dc (*UKtr*) cluster.

Round 4: sl st into next 2 ch sp, work *4dc (*UKtr*) cluster, 1 ch* into each 2 ch sp, join with a sl st to top of first 4dc (*UKtr*) cluster.

Round 5: repeat round 4.

Round 6: sl st into next 2 ch sp, *3dc (*UKtr*) cluster, 1 sc (*UKdc*)* into each 2 ch sp, join with a sl st to top of 3dc (*UKtr*) cluster.

Round 7: sl st into next 2 ch sp, work a 3dc (*UKtr*) cluster into the 1 ch at the top of each 3dc (*UKtr*) cluster of the previous round, but omit the 1 ch to secure, join as previous round.

Making up

Carefully push tiny pieces of stuffing inside the pine cone using the crochet hook to help you. Do not overstuff – just get a pleasing shape.

Using a small amount of craft glue, attach the holly berry embellishment to the top of the pine cone. Thread ribbon through the last row of clusters. Decide how long you want the ribbon loop to be and trim the ribbon as necessary. Either tie the ends of the ribbon together in a knot or stitch them with a needle and gold thread to form a loop.

These lovely little flowers work in all sorts of colour combinations. Use them to decorate cushions, lampshades and throws around the home.

PINK COSMOS

Materials:
Small amounts of No. 3 crochet cotton in lime green,
  pale green and bright pink; 100g/306yd/280m

Hook:
Size 3mm (US D, UK 10) crochet hook

Instructions:

With lime green crochet cotton, make an adjustable ring
(see page 21).

Round 1: 2 ch, sc (*UKdc*) into ring eight times. Fasten off
the lime green yarn.

Change to pale green yarn and sl st together.

Round 2: 2 ch, hdc (*UKhtr*) into each sc (*UKdc*)
eight times, 1 hdc (*UKhtr*) into base ch of 2
ch, join in bright pink and sl st into 2 ch.

Make the petal cluster:

*2 ch, 1 dc (*UKtr*), 1 tr (*UKdtr*), 1 dc
(*UKtr*), 2 ch, sl st, all into first ch
of 2-ch, hdc (*UKhtr*), sc (*UKdc*)
into next hdc (*UKhtr*)*, repeat
from * to * eight more times
(making 9 petals in total).

Fasten off and weave in
all loose ends.

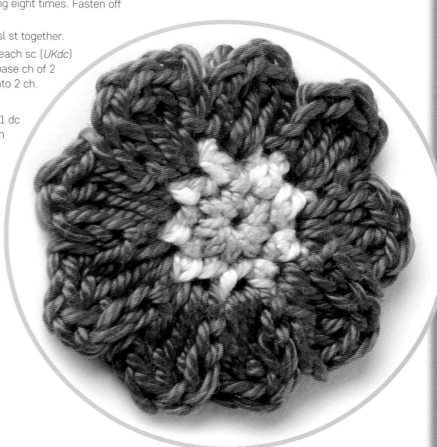

TEDDY BEAR

Note

When working the pieces, it is a good idea to mark the beginning of each round to avoid losing or even gaining stitches. Stuff each part with small amounts of filling as you work; avoid over-stuffing.

Gauge (tension)

5 sc (*UKdc*) measure 1in (2.5cm) in width using the stated hook, though gauge (tension) is not critical as the finished size of the bear is only approximate.

Instructions:

Head

Round 1: with the appropriate colour yarn, make 2 ch, 6 sc (*UKdc*) in 2nd ch from hook, join in a circle with a sl st.

Round 2: 1 ch, 2 sc (*UKdc*) in each sc (*UKdc*) all round, join with a sl st (12 sts).

Rounds 3–5: work in sc (*UKdc*).

Join the contrasting yarn, if stated in the instructions, and proceed as follows:

Round 6: *1 sc (*UKdc*) in next sc (*UKdc*), 2 sc (*UKdc*) in next sc (*UKdc*)*, rep from * to * all round.

Rounds 7 and 8: work in sc (*UKdc*).

Round 9: inc 6 sc (*UKdc*) evenly in round.

Rounds 10–15: work in sc (*UKdc*).

Round 16: dec 6 sc (*UKdc*) evenly in round.

Round 17: work in sc (*UKdc*).

Round 18: dec 6 sc (*UKdc*) evenly in round.

Round 19: work in sc (*UKdc*).

Round 20: dec 4 sc (*UKdc*) evenly in round.

Break yarn and run through last round. Draw up and fasten off.

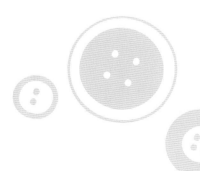

Body

Round 1: with the appropriate colour yarn, make 2 ch, work 6 sc (*UKdc*) in 2nd ch from hook, join with a sl st to form a tight circle.

Subsequent rounds are all joined with a sl st unless otherwise stated.

Round 2: 2 sc (*UKdc*) in each dc (*UKdc*) all round, join as before (12 sts).

Round 3: *1 sc (*UKdc*) in next st, 2 sc (*UKdc*) in next sc (*UKdc*)*, rep from * to * all round (18 sts).

Round 4: *1 sc (*UKdc*) in each of next 2 sc (*UKdc*), 2 sc (*UKdc*) in next sc (*UKdc*)*, rep from * to * all round (24 sts).

Round 5: *1 sc (*UKdc*) in each of next 3 sc (*UKdc*), 2 sc (*UKdc*) in next sc (*UKdc*)*, rep from * to * all round (30 sts).

Rounds 6–18: sc (*UKdc*).

Round 19: dec 6 sts evenly all round (24 sts).

Round 20: sc (*UKdc*).

Rep rounds 19 and 20 until 6 sc (*UKdc*) rem.

Finish stuffing the body, break yarn and run the thread through the last round. Draw up and fasten off.

Arms (make 2)

Round 1: with the appropriate colour yarn, make 2 ch, 7 sc (*UKdc*) in 2nd ch from hook, join in a tight circle with a sl st.

Round 2: 2 sc (*UKdc*) in each st, 14 sc (*UKdc*), join with a sl st.

Rounds 3–14: sc (*UKdc*).

Round 15: *sc (*UKdc*) 2 tog, 1 sc (*UKdc*) in next sc (*UKdc*)*, rep from * to * all round.

Round 16: sc (*UKdc*) all round. Break yarn.

Complete the stuffing, pushing a little extra into the base of the arm to form the paw. Pull up to close.
This is the top of the arm.

Legs (make 2)

The foot is shaped, so push a little extra stuffing into that area as you work.

Round 1: with the appropriate colour yarn, make 2 ch, 7 sc (*UKdc*) in 2nd ch from hook, join in a tight circle with a sl st.

Round 2: 2 sc (*UKdc*) in each st, 14 sc (*UKdc*), join with a sl st.

Round 3: *1 sc (*UKdc*), 2 sc (*UKdc*) in next st*, rep from * to *, working 1 sc (*UKdc*) in last st (20 sts).

Rounds 4–6: sc (*UKdc*) all round.

Round 7: 7 sc (*UKdc*), (sc (*UKdc*) 2 tog) three times, 7 sc (*UKdc*).

Rounds 8–17: sc (*UKdc*) all round.

Round 18: dec 3 sts evenly all round.

Round 19: sc (*UKdc*) all round.

Round 20: dec 3 sts evenly all round.

Break yarn, draw yarn through last round of sc (*UKdc*), draw up and fasten off.

Ears (make 2)

Round 1: with the appropriate colour yarn, make 2 ch, 7 sc (*UKdc*) in 2nd ch from hook, join into a circle.

Round 2: 2 sc (*UKdc*) in each sc (*UKdc*) all round.

Round 3: sc (*UKdc*) all round. Fasten off.

Making up

Work in all the loose ends. Sew the head firmly to the body. You can position the head at different angles to give the bear more character. Pin the ears on each side of the head, and when you are happy with their position, sew them on firmly. Embroider the nose and eyes on to the head of the bear, then stitch a straight line from the centre of the nose to the chin, and a thin line above the eyes to make the eyebrows. Sew the arms in position on either side of the bear's shoulders. Attach the legs, one on each side, in a sitting position. Make sure they are level so that your bear sits down properly.

HEART COASTERS

Materials:

Small amounts of light worsted (DK/8-ply) cotton yarn in variations of pale blue (A) and navy (B) or variations of these plus cream and mid-blue; 50g/93yd/85m

Hook:

Size 4mm (US 6, UK 8) crochet hook

Size:

From bottom point to centre top between lobes: 4½in (11cm)

Instructions:

Using yarn A, ch 2, work 3 sc (*UKdc*) in second ch from hook (3 sts).

Row 1: 1 ch, 1 sc (*UKdc*) in each st (3 sts).

Row 2: 1 ch, 2 sc (*UKdc*) in first st, 1 sc (UKdc), 2 sc (*UKdc*) into last st (5 sts).

Row 3: 1 ch, 2 sc (*UKdc*) in first st, 3 sc (UKdc), 2 sc (*UKdc*) into last st (7 sts).

Row 4: 1 ch, sc (*UKdc*) into each st (7 sts).

Row 5: 1 ch, 2 sc (*UKdc*) in first st, 5 sc (UKdc), 2 sc (*UKdc*) into last st (9 sts).

Row 6: 1 ch, sc (*UKdc*) into each st (9 sts).

Row 7: 1 ch, 2 sc (*UKdc*) into first st, 7 sc (UKdc), 2 sc (*UKdc*) into last st (11 sts).

Row 8: 1 ch 1, sc (*UKdc*) into each st (11 sts).

Row 9: 1 ch, 2 sc (*UKdc*) into first st, 9 sc (UKdc), 2 sc (*UKdc*) into last st (13 sts).

Row 10: 1 ch, 2 sc (*UKdc*) into first st, 11 sc (*UKdc*), 2 sc (*UKdc*) into last st (15 sts).

Row 11: 1 ch, 2 sc (*UKdc*) into first st, 13 sc (*UKdc*), 2 sc (*UKdc*) into last st (17 sts).

Rows 12 and 13: 1 ch 1, sc (*UKdc*) into each st (17 sts).

Row 14: 1 ch, 2 sc (*UKdc*) in first st, 15 sc (UKdc), 2 sc (*UKdc*) in last st (19 sts).

Row 15: 1 ch 1, sc (*UKdc*) into each st (19 sts).

Row 16: 1 ch, 2 sc (*UKdc*) in first st, 17 sc (*UKdc*), 2 sc (*UKdc*) in last st (21 sts).

Row 17: 1 ch, sc (*UKdc*) into each st (21 sts).

Rght lobe

Row 18: 1 ch, 10 sc (*UKdc*), turn (10 sts).

Row 19: 1 ch, sc (*UKdc*)2tog, sc (UKdc) in each st (9 sts).

Row 20: 1 ch, sc (*UKdc*)2tog, sc (*UKdc*) to last 2 sts, sc (*UKdc*)2tog (7 sts).

Row 21: 1 ch, sc (*UKdc*)2tog, sc (*UKdc*) to last 2 sts, sc (*UKdc*)2tog (5 sts).

Row 22: 1 ch, sc (*UKdc*)2tog, sc (*UKdc*) to last 2 sts, sc (*UKdc*)2tog (3 sts).

Fasten off.

Left lobe

Row 23: Rejoin yarn A to tenth st from left (there will be one unworked st in the middle), 1 ch, 10 sc (*UKdc*), turn (10 sts).

Row 24: 1 ch, sc (*UKdc*) to last 2 sts, sc (*UKdc*)2tog (9 sts).

Row 25: 1 ch, sc (*UKdc*)2tog, sc (*UKdc*) to last 2 sts, sc (*UKdc*)2tog (7 sts).

Row 26: 1 ch, sc (*UKdc*)2tog, sc (*UKdc*) to last 2 sts, sc (*UKdc*)2tog (5 sts).

Row 27: 1 ch, sc (*UKdc*)2tog, sc (*UKdc*) to last 2 sts, sc (*UKdc*)2tog (3 sts).

Fasten off.

Edging

Join yarn B to the right of the bottom point, ch 1, sc (*UKdc*) in each st around. You may need to work 2 sc (*UKdc*) into one or two sts on the curves of the heart lobes so that the yarn is not too tight. At the bottom point, work [1sc (*UKdc*), 1hdc (*UKhtr*), 1 sc (*UKdc*)] into the centre st, sl st to initial ch.

Fasten off and weave in all loose ends.

CLEMATIS

Materials:

Small amounts of No. 3 crochet cotton in mid-green (A), fuchsia (B) and pink (C); 100g/280m/306yd

Hook:

Size 2.5mm (US B/1, UK 13) crochet hook

Size:

Approx. 6in (15cm) from outer petal tip to opposite outer petal tip

Instructions:

Using yarn A, make an adjustable ring (see page 21), ch 1, 12 sc (*UKdc*) in ring, join with a sl st into first ch to form a ring. Pull tail of yarn to close circle.

Round 1: 1 ch, 1 sc (*UKdc*) in same stitch, *1 sc (*UKdc*) in next stitch, 12 ch, 1 sc (*UKdc*) in same stitch, 1 sc (*UKdc*) in next stitch, 1 ch, 1 sc (*UKdc*) in next stitch, repeat from * to last sc (*UKdc*), join with sl st into first sc (*UKdc*) (four 12-ch loops). Fasten off.

Round 2: Join yarn B to any loop, *9 tr (*UKdtr*), 2 dtr (*UKtrtr*), 9 tr (*UKdtr*) into the 12-ch loop, sl st into 1-ch space from round 1, rep from * to end, join with a sl st to first ch. Fasten off.

Round 3: Join yarn C to sp between st 10 and st 11 of any petal, *12 ch, sl st into st between petals, 12 ch, sl st between st 10 and st 11 of next petal, rep from * to end, sl st to top of first petal.

Round 4: 3 ch, 11 dc (*UKtr*) in 12-ch sp, *2 ch, 12 dc (*UKtr*) in next 12-ch sp, rep from * to end, 2 ch, sl st in third ch of initial ch-3.

Making up

Fasten off and weave in all ends. Block carefully to shape.

Opposite:

To make this attractive table runner, make eight motifs in the colours of your choice and block them carefully. Arrange the motifs in a colour scheme that you are happy with, then choose one colour with which to join them together. With RS facing, join the first two motifs by using a tapestry needle to stitch through the back loops only of 4 sts where the two petals meet. Fasten off the yarn. Continue along the middle until you have joined the eight motifs along the centre of the finished piece. Next, join the side petals together in the same way. Weave in loose ends, or knot and cut yarn close to the knot.

WATERMELON

Materials:

1 ball each of worsted weight (light aran) yarn in deep rose (A), white (B) and green (C); 100g/220yd/200m

Notions:

Approx. 111 x small black beads

6¾in (17cm) zip

Hook:

4.5mm (US 7, UK 7) crochet hook

Size:

Approx. 3½in (9cm) end to end and 7½in (19cm) at the widest point

Instructions:

Thread all the beads onto yarn A and with 4.5mm (US 7, UK 7) crochet hook make 6 hdc (UKhtr) in adjustable ring (see page 21). Join with a sl st to first st.

Work a bead into every other hdc (UKhtr) on rounds: 1, 3, 5, 7 and 9 only.

Round 1: 2 ch (count as 1 hdc (UKhtr)), 1 hdc (UKhtr) into base of 2 ch, *2 hdc (UKhtr) in next st, rep from * to end, sl st into second ch at beg of round (12 sts).

Round 2: 2 ch (count as 1 hdc (UKhtr)), 1 hdc (UKhtr) into base of 2 ch, *1 hdc (UKhtr) in next st, 2 hdc (UKhtr) in next st, rep from * to last st, 1 hdc (UKhtr) into last st, sl st into second ch at beg of round (18 sts).

Round 3: 2 ch (count as 1 hdc (UKhtr)), 1 hdc (UKhtr) in next st, 2 hdc (UKhtr) in next st, *1 hdc (UKhtr) in next 2 sts, 2 hdc (UKhtr) in next st, rep from * to end, sl st into second ch at beg of round (24 sts).

Round 4: 2 ch (count as 1 hdc (UKhtr)), 1 hdc (UKhtr) in next 2 sts, 2 hdc (UKhtr) in next st, *1 hdc (UKhtr) in next 3 sts, 2 hdc (UKhtr) in next st, rep from * to end, sl st into second ch at beg of round (30 sts).

Round 5: 2 ch (count as 1 hdc (UKhtr)), 1 hdc (UKhtr) in next 2 sts, 2 hdc (UKhtr) in next st, *1 hdc (UKhtr) in next 3 sts, 2 hdc (UKhtr) in next st, rep from * to last 2 sts, 1 hdc (UKhtr) in next 2 sts, sl st into second ch at beg of round (37 sts).

Round 6: 2 ch (count as 1 hdc (UKhtr)), 1 hdc (UKhtr) in next 2 sts, 2 hdc (UKhtr) in next st, *1 hdc (UKhtr) in next 3 sts, 2 hdc (UKhtr) in next st, rep from * to last st, 1 hdc (UKhtr), sl st into second ch at beg of round (46 sts).

Round 7: 2 ch (count as 1 hdc (UKhtr)), 1 hdc (UKhtr) in next 2 sts, 2 hdc (UKhtr) in next st, *1 hdc (UKhtr) in next 3 sts, 2 hdc (UKhtr) in next st, rep from * to last 2 sts, 1 hdc (UKhtr) in next 2 sts, sl st into second ch at beg of round (57 sts).

Round 8: 2 ch (count as 1 hdc (UKhtr)), 1 hdc (UKhtr) in next 2 sts, 2 hdc (UKhtr) in next st, *1 hdc (UKhtr) in next 3 sts, 2 hdc (UKhtr) in next st, rep from * to last st, 1 hdc (UKhtr), sl st into second ch at beg of round (71 sts).

Round 9: 2 ch (count as 1 hdc (UKhtr)), 1 hdc (UKhtr) in next 2 sts, 2 hdc (UKhtr) in next st, *1 hdc (UKhtr) in next 3 sts, 2 hdc (UKhtr) in next st, rep from * to last 3 sts, 1 hdc (UKhtr) in next 3 sts, sl st into second ch at beg of round (88 sts).

Round 10: 2 ch (count as 1 hdc (UKhtr)), 1 hdc (UKhtr) in every st to end, sl st into second ch at beg of round. Change to yarn B.

Round 11: 2 ch (count as 1 hdc (UKhtr)), 1 hdc (UKhtr) in every st to end, sl st into second ch at beg of round. Change to yarn C.

Round 12: 2 ch (count as 1 hdc (UKhtr)), 1 hdc (UKhtr) in every st to end, sl st into second ch at beg of round.

Fasten off yarn.

Making up

Weave in ends. Fold purse in half and stitch for 2in (5cm) up each side. Insert the zip.

POPPIES & DAISIES

Materials:

Small amounts of No. 3 crochet cotton in yellow (A), white (B), green (C) and dark green (D); 100g/306yd/280m

Hook:

Size 3mm (US D, UK 10)

Size:

3½in (9cm) diameter

Instructions:

Using A, 6 ch, join into a circle with a sl st.

Round 1: 5 ch [counts as first dc (*UKtr*) and ch sp], *1 dc (*UKtr*) into circle, 2 ch*, rep from * to * six more times, join with sl st to 3rd of 5 ch at beg of round (8 x 2 ch sp). Break A.

Round 2: using B, sl st into first 2 ch sp, 3 ch, work 4 dc (*UKtr*) into sp but keeping last loop of each dc (*UKtr*) on hook, yrh, draw through all loops on hook [5 dc (*UKtr*) cluster made], 4 ch, *5 dc (*UKtr*) cluster in next sp, 4 ch*, rep from * to * all round, join with a sl st to top of first cluster at beg of round. Break B.

Round 3: using C, 1 ch, 1 sc (*UKdc*) into top of cluster, *3 ch, 1 long dc (*UKtr*) into top of dc (*UKtr*) on 2nd round, 3 ch, 1 sc (*UKdc*) into top of next 5 dc (*UKtr*) cluster*, rep from * to * all round, ending 3 ch, sl st to top of 5 dc (*UKtr*) cluster at beg of round. Break C.

Round 4: using D, sl st into first 3 ch sp, 3 ch, [3 dc (*UKtr*), 3 ch, 4 dc (*UKtr*)] into same sp, *3 dc (*UKtr*) into each of next three 3 ch sp, [[4 dc (*UKtr*), 3 ch, 4 dc (*UKtr*)] into next 3 ch sp*, rep from * to * twice more, 3 dc (*UKtr*) into each of next three 3 ch sp, sl st into top of 3 ch at beg of round. Fasten off.

Weave in all loose ends.

Special abbreviations

5 dc (*UKtr*) cluster: work 5 dc (*UKtr*) into next sp keeping last loop of each dc (*UKtr*) on hook, yrh, draw through all loops on hook.

Long dc (*UKtr*): work dc (*UKtr*) as normal but pull up a longer loop of yarn as you do so.

Materials:

1 ball each of sport weight
(6-ply) wool/acrylic blend
yarn in cherry and marine
blue; 50g/137yd/125m

Hook:

Size 5mm (US H/8, UK 6)
crochet hook

Size:

Head circumference 21¼–23in
(54–58cm)

Gauge (tension) sample

17 sts and 22 rounds of sc (*UK dc*)
using a 5mm (US H/8, UK 6) crochet
hook = 4 x 4in (10 x 10cm). Change
your hook if necessary to obtain the
correct gauge (tension).

Colour pattern

Rounds 1–40: Crochet alternately
four rounds in cherry, and four
rounds in marine blue. When
changing colour, draw in the new
colour on the last st of the previous
round to achieve a perfect colour
transition (see page 22).

Rounds 41–50: Crochet alternately
two rounds in cherry, and two
rounds in marine blue.

Sc (*UKdc*) in spiral rounds

Work sc (*UK dc*) in rounds like
spirals, marking the start of the
round with a contrasting thread
(see page 21).

SAILOR GIRL BEANIE

Instructions:

Start the beanie at the crown and work down to the bottom edge in spiral rounds of sc (*UKdc*) as explained on page 21.

Begin with 2 ch in cherry.

Round 1: Work 6 sc (*UKdc*) into the 2nd ch from the hook (see page 21). Mark the start of the row with contrasting yarn.

Round 2 (cherry): 2 sc (*UKdc*) in every st around (12 sts).

Round 3 (cherry): Work * 1 sc (*UKdc*) then 2 sc (*UKdc*) in next st * , rep from * to * around (18 sts).

Round 4 (cherry): Work * sc (*UKdc*) in each of next 2 sts then 2 sc (*UKdc*) in next st * , rep from * to * around (24 sts).

Round 5 (blue): Work * sc (*UKdc*) in each of next 3 sts then 2 sc (*UKdc*) in next st * , rep from * to * around (30 sts).

Round 6 (blue): Work * sc (*UKdc*) in each of next 4 sts then 2 sc (*UKdc*) in next st * , rep from * to * around (36 sts).

Round 7 (blue): Work * sc (*UKdc*) in each of next 5 sts then 2 sc (*UKdc*) in next st * , rep from * to * around (42 sts).

Round 8 (blue): Work sc (*UKdc*) in every st around (42 sts).

Round 9 (cherry): Work * sc (*UKdc*) in each of next 6 sts then 2 sc (*UKdc*) in next st * , rep from * to * around (48 sts).

Round 10 (cherry): Work * sc (*UKdc*) in each of next 7 sts then 2 sc (*UKdc*) in next st * , rep from * to * around (54 sts).

Round 11 (cherry): Work * sc (*UKdc*) in each of next 8 sts then 2 sc (*UKdc*) in next st * , rep from * to * around (60 sts).

Round 12 (cherry): Work sc (*UKdc*) in every st around (60 sts).

Continue increasing in this way until the end of round 24, changing colour after every 4 rounds and not making any increases on the last round of each colour. Round 24 has 114 sts.

Round 25 (cherry): Work * sc (*UKdc*) in each of next 18 sts then 2 sc (*UKdc*) in next st * , rep from * to * around (120 sts).

Rounds 26–39: Work sc (*UKdc*) in every st around (120 sts).

Round 40 (blue): Work * sc, sc2tog (*UKdc, dc2tog*) * , rep from * to * around (80 sts).

Rounds 41–45: From now on, alternate colours every 2 rounds. Work sc (*UKdc*) in every st around (80 sts).

Round 46 (cherry): Work * sc (*UKdc*) in each of the next 6 sts then sc2tog (*UKdc2tog*) * , rep from * to * around (70 sts).

Rounds 47–48 (blue): Work sc (*UKdc*) in every st around (70 sts).

Round 49 (cherry): Work sc (*UKdc*) in every st around then join into a round with a sl st.

Round 50: Still using cherry yarn, work into each st around in rev sc (*UKrev dc*) as explained on page 23.

Fasten off and weave in all loose ends.

FESTIVE WREATH

Materials:

- 1 ball each of No. 5 crochet cotton in dark green and light green; 100g/437yd/400m
- 3 small holly berry embellishments
- 20in (0.5m) of narrow green satin ribbon
- Gold ribbon bow or a short length of gold ribbon to tie in a bow
- Gold bell

Craft glue

Green sewing thread (optional)

Tools:

Size 2mm (US B/1, UK 14) crochet hook

Sewing needle

Size:

Approx. 2¾in (7cm) in diameter

Instructions:

Using light green crochet cotton, make 50 ch.

Row 1: Work 2 dc (*UKtr*) into 3rd ch from hook, 3 dc (*UKtr*) into each ch to end. As you work, the crochet will twirl into a tight corkscrew shape.

Use dark green cotton to make another twist in the same way.

Making up

Secure both the light green and dark green crochet twists together at one end, then twine the strips around each other, folding the coils inside one another as you do so, until you get a neat double coil. Join the two ends together firmly.

Glue the holly berry embellishments on the coil at random, tucking them inside the twists. Glue the ribbon bow and bell at the top of the wreath to cover the join where the ends of the twists meet.

Thread the ribbon through the top of the wreath to make a hanging loop. Decide how long you want the ribbon loop to be and trim the ribbon as necessary. Either tie the ends of the ribbon together in a knot or stitch them to form a loop.

GAZANIA

Instructions:

Using colour A, make an adjustable ring (see page 21).

Round 1: 1 ch, 10 sc (*UKdc*) into ring. Pull end to close ring.

Fasten off colour A and change to colour B.

sl st into first sc (*UKdc*) of ring.

Round 2: 6 ch, sl st into base ch, *sc (*UKdc*) into next sc (*UKdc*) of ring, 5 ch, sl st into base sc (*UKdc*)*, repeat from * to * nine times, making ten petals in total.

Fasten off colour B and change to colour C.

Round 3: insert hook into base ch of first petal.

sl st, 7 ch, *sl st into base sc (*UKdc*) between petals 1 and 2, 6 ch*, repeat from * to * between each petal base, sc (*UKdc*) nine times, sl st into base of first petal.

Fasten off colour C and weave in all loose ends.

Materials:
Small amounts of No. 3 crochet cotton in yellow (A), purple (B) and white (C); 100g/306yd/280m

Hook:
Size 2.5mm (US B/1, UK 13) crochet hook

53

Add a splash of colour to an otherwise plain pair of slippers with these fanciful flowers.

SWEET ANGEL BEAR

Materials:

1 ball of No. 5 crochet cotton in pale blue, and small amounts in mid-blue, black, pale turquoise and white; 100g/437yd/400m

Small amount of silver metallic yarn

Black floss for embroidering features

Short length of silver jewellery wire

Toy stuffing

Sewing threads to match crochet cotton

Tools:

Size 2.5mm (US B/1, UK 13) crochet hook

Sewing needle

Instructions:

Make the bear following the instructions on page 37, using pale blue for the head, body, arms and legs and mid-blue for the muzzle and ears.

Wings (make 4)

Row 1: Using white crochet cotton, make 3 ch, 9 dc (UKtr) in 3rd ch from hook, turn.

Row 2: 3 ch, 1 dc (UKtr) in first dc (UKtr), 2 dc (UKtr) in each of rem dc (UKtr), turn.

Row 3: 1 sc (UKdc) in each dc (UKtr) to end.

Break white and join in metallic yarn. Work a further row of sc (UKdc) round the edge of the wing. Fasten off.

Skirt

Round 1: using pale turquoise, make 30 ch. Join with a sl st to beg of round, making sure you do not twist the chain.

Round 2: 1 ch, 1 sc (UKdc) in each ch to end, joining as before.

Round 3: 4 ch, skip 2 sc (UKdc), 1 sc (UKdc) in next sc (UKdc), *2 ch, skip 2 ch, 1 sc (UKdc) in next sc (UKdc)*. Rep from * to * all round, 2 ch, sl st to 2nd of 4 turning ch of previous round. Change to white yarn.

Round 4: sl st in first ch sp, 3 ch, [1 dc (UKtr), 2 ch, 2 dc (UKtr)] in same sp, *[2 dc (UKtr), 2 ch, 2 dc (UKtr)] in next sp*, rep from * to * all round, join in top of 3 ch at beg of round.

Round 5: rep round 4.

Round 6: change to pale turquoise and work round 5 again. Fasten off.

Join in silver metallic yarn and work edging as follows:

Round 7: *1 sc (UKdc) in each of next 2 dc (UKtr), picot in next sp, (3 ch, sl st in first of the 3 ch)*, rep from * to * all round, join with a sl st.

Halo

Round 1: Make 10 ch, join in a ring with a sl st, *5 ch, 1 sc (UKdc)*, rep from * to * eight times, join with a sl st to beg of round.

Round 2: *5 sc (UKdc) in 5 ch loop, sl st in next sc (UKdc)*, rep from * to * all round, join with a sl st to beg of round. Fasten off.

Making up

Work in the ends on all the pieces. Sew the wings together in pairs. Join them in the centre and place them on the bear's back level with the tops of the arms. Sew them firmly in place. Slip the skirt on to the bear with the join at centre back. Secure with a few stitches. Take a length of silver jewellery wire and thread it around the inner edge of the halo. Twist the ends of the wire together and push them firmly in the bear's head towards the back. Arrange the halo in a pleasing shape.

HEART STRING

Materials

Small amounts of light worsted (DK/8-ply) yarn in maroon, pink and mushroom; 50g/142yd/130m

Sewing thread

Toy stuffing

Tools:

Size 4mm (US 6, UK 8) crochet hook

Sewing needle

Notions:

8 small bell beads

3 hanging decorations in toning colours

Size:

23¼in (59cm) from top of loop to bottom of hanging decoration

Instructions

Make 2 for each heart

Round 1: With yarn colour of your choice, make an adjustable ring (see page 21), ch 3, and work into the ring 6 sc (UKdc), 1 dc (UKtr), 6 sc (UKdc), 3ch, sl st. Gently pull the tail end of the yarn to close the ring (but leave a small gap, as your final sl st will be made into the centre) and the heart shape will appear.

Round 2: 3 ch, skip the 3-ch from previous round, 3 sc (UKdc) into the first st, 1 sc (UKdc) in each of the next 2 sts, 1 hdc (UKhtr) in each of the next 3 sts, [1 dc (UKtr), 1 tr (UKdtr), 1 dc (UKtr)] into the next st (this is the bottom point of the heart), 1 hdc (UKhtr) in each of the next 3 sts, 1 sc (UKdc) in each of the next 2 sts, 3 sc (UKdc) in the last st, ch 3 and sl st in the centre of the heart.

Edging

First, tug the yarn tail again to make sure the centre hole is closed properly, as you will now be stuffing the heart. This will prevent any toy stuffing poking through.

Holding two hearts tog with WS facing, join yarn to the right of the bottom point, ch 1 and sc (UKdc) in each st through both layers. You may need to work 2 sc (UKdc) into one or two sts on the curves of the heart lobes so that the stitches do not pull. At the bottom point of the heart, work 1 sc (UKdc), 1 dc (UKtr), 1 sc (UKdc) into the middle st, then sl st into initial ch. Fasten off and weave in all loose ends.

Making up

Choose a colour for the hanging chain and connect the six hearts tog by joining yarn to the middle of the heart lobes, make 6 ch and join to bottom point of next heart. Repeat to join all hearts tog. To make the hanging loop, join yarn to the middle of the heart lobes on the top heart, make 16 ch and rejoin to the middle. Fasten off.

Sew a bell bead to the bottom of the top five hearts, and three to the bottom of the last heart. Attach some hanging decorations with gold and maroon beads to the bottom heart with some yarn.

LILY

Materials:
Small amounts of No. 3 crochet cotton in
fuchsia (A), purple (B) and pale green (C);
100g/306yd/280m

Size:
Approx. 4in (10cm) from petal tip to
opposite petal tip

Hook:
Size 2.5mm (US B/1, UK 13) crochet hook

Stitch note

The picot stitch is worked as
follows: work 2 ch, sl st into second
ch from hook.

Instructions:

Using yarn A, make an adjustable
ring (see page 21), ch 1, work 18
sc (UKdc) into ring, join with sl st to
first st to form a ring. Fasten off.

Round 1: Join B to any st, *1 ch, skip
1 st, sl st to next st, 12 ch, sl st to
next st, rep from * to end (six 12-ch
loops).

Round 2: Work into first loop: *6 dc
(UKtr), 1 picot, 6 dc (UKtr), sl st to st
before next loop, rep from * to end.
Fasten off. (6 petals)

Round 3: Working behind petals,
join C to st at bottom middle of any
petal, 3 ch, *sl st to bottom middle
of next petal, 3 ch rep from * four
times, join to first st (6 loops).

Round 4: sl st to first loop, [3 ch, 2
dc (UKtr), 2 ch, 3 dc (UKtr), 1 ch] in
same loop, in next loop work *[3 dc
(UKtr), 2 ch, 3 dc (UKtr), 1 ch], rep
from * four times, sl st to third ch of
initial 3-ch.

Round 5: sl st to corner sp, work [3
ch, 2 dc (UKtr), 2 ch, 3 dc (UKtr), 1
ch] in same sp, along each side ch-
sp work [3 dc (UKtr), 1 ch], in corner
ch-sps work [3 dc (UKtr), 2 ch, 3 dc
(UKtr), 1 ch]. At end sl st in third ch
of 3-ch.

Making up

Fasten off and weave in all loose
ends. Block to achieve the correct
hexagonal shape and pin the petals
out carefully to close the centre
gaps a little.

*You can make this motif in lots of bright colours to mimic
real lilies. With the addition of a crocheted or elastic
band, this flower would make a pretty headband.*

ARIA PURSE

Materials:

1 ball of mohair and silk lace weight (2-ply) yarn in white (A); 25g/229yd/210m

1 ball of alpaca and merino lace weight (2-ply) yarn in white (B); 50g/437yd/400m

1 round piece of lining fabric 5½in (14cm) in diameter and 1 rectangular piece 6 x 12¼in (15 x 31cm)

Hook:

4mm (US 6, UK 8) crochet hook

Notions:

2 x large beads

Size:

Approx. 5¼in (13cm) in diameter and 7½in (19cm) high

Pattern note

Use one strand of A and one of B held together throughout.

Instructions:

With yarn A and B held together, make 6 ch, join with sl st to first ch to form a ring.

Round 1: 1 ch, work 12 sc (UKdc) into ring, sl st to first st (12 sts).

Round 2: 1 ch, 2 sc (UKdc) in every st to end, sl st to first st (24 sts).

Round 3: 1 ch, *1 sc (UKdc) in next st, 2 sc (UKdc) in next st, rep from * to end, sl st to first st (36 sts).

Round 4 and 5: 1 ch, 1 sc (UKdc) in every st to end, sl st to first st.

Round 6: 1 ch, *1 sc (UKdc) in next 2 sts, 2 sc (UKdc) in next st, rep from * to end, sl st to first st (48 sts).

Round 7: 1 ch, 1 sc (UKdc) in every st to end, sl st to first st.

Round 8: 1 ch, *1 sc (UKdc) in next 3 sts, 2 sc (UKdc) in next st, rep from * to end, sl st to first st (60 sts).

Round 9: As round 7.

Round 10: 1 ch,*1 sc (UKdc) in next 4 sts, 2 sc (UKdc) in next st, rep from * to end, sl st to first st (72 sts).

Round 11: As round 7.

Round 12: 1 ch, *1 sc (UKdc) in next 5 sts, 2 sc (UKdc) in next st, rep from * to end, sl st to first st (84 sts).

Round 13: As round 7.

Start of lace pattern

Round 1: 3 ch, (counts as 1 dc (UKtr)), 2 dc (UKtr) in st at the base of 3 ch, skip 2 sts, 1 sc (UKdc) in next st, 5 ch, skip 5 sts, 1 sc (UKdc) in next st, *skip 2 sts, 5 dc (UKtr) in next st, skip 2 sts, 1 sc (UKdc) in next st, 5 ch, skip 5 sts, 1 sc (UKdc) in next st, rep from * to last 2 sts, skip 2 sts, 2 dc (UKtr) in st at base of beg 3 ch, sl st to third ch at beg of round.

Round 2: 1 ch, 1 sc (UKdc) in first dc (UKtr), *5 ch, 1 sc (UKdc) in next ch sp, 5 ch, 1 sc (UKdc) in third of next 5 dc (UKtr), rep from * five times more, 5 ch, 1 sc (UKdc) in next ch sp, 5 ch, sl st to first sc (UKdc).

Round 3: *5 ch, 1 sc (UKdc) in next ch sp, 5 dc (UKtr) in next dc, 1 sc (UKdc) in next ch sp, rep from * six times more, 3 ch, sl st to third ch at beg of round.

Round 4: 1 ch, 1 sc (UKdc) in base of 1 ch, *5 ch, 1 sc (UKdc) in third of next 5 dc (UKtr), 5 ch, 1 sc (UKdc) in next ch sp, rep from * five times

more, 5 ch, 1 sc (UKdc) in third of next 5 dc (UKtr), 5 ch, sl st to first sc (UKdc).

Round 5: 3 ch (counts as 1 dc (UKtr)), 2 dc (UKtr) in sc (UKdc) at base of ch, 1 sc (UKdc) in next ch sp, ch 5, 1 sc (UKdc) in next ch sp, *5 dc (UKtr) in next sc (UKdc), 1 sc (UKdc) in next ch sp, 5 ch, 1 sc (UKdc) in next ch sp, rep from * five times more, 2 dc (UKtr) in st at base of 3 ch, sl st to third ch at beg of round.

Rep rounds 2–5 three more times, then rounds 2 and 3 once. Fasten off yarn.

Ties (make 2)

With yarn A and B held together and 4mm (US G/6, UK 8) crochet hook, make 60 ch.

Fasten off yarn.

Making up

Weave in all loose ends and sew the lining in place, leaving a ½in (1cm) seam allowance. Thread ties (from opposite directions) into round 6 of the pattern from the top, bring each pair of ends out (again at opposite sides), thread the beads on and tie a knot in each end.

SQUARE DANCE

Materials:

Small amounts of No. 3 crochet cotton in
  cream (A), pale blue (B) and royal blue (C);
  100g/306yd/280m

2 small matching buttons

Matching thread and sewing needle

Hook:

Size 3mm (US D, UK 10)
crochet hook

Size:

2¼in (6cm) across

63

Instructions:

Using A, make 8 ch, join into a ring with a sl st.

Round 1: work 1 ch, 12 sc (*UKdc*) into a ring, join with
a sl st.

Round 2: 3 ch, 1 dc (*UKtr*) into same sp as 3 ch, 2 dc
(*UKtr*) into each sc (*UKdc*) to end, join to 3 ch at beg of
round, 24 dc (*UKtr*). Fasten off yarn A.

Round 3: using B, work 4 ch, skip 2 dc (*UKtr*), 1 dc (*UKtr*)
into sp, 1 ch, skip 2 dc (*UKtr*), **7 dc (*UKtr*) into next sp,
*1 ch, skip 2 dc (*UKtr*), 1 dc (*UKtr*) into sp between next
2 dc (*UKtr*)*, rep from * to * once more,
1 ch, skip 2 dc (*UKtr*)**, rep from ** to ** twice more, 6
dc (*UKtr*) into same sp as 4 ch at beg of round, join with
a sl st to 3rd of 4 ch. Fasten off yarn B.

Round 4: using C, **[*1 ch, 1 sc (*UKdc*) in next sp*,
rep from * to * twice more, 1 ch, skip 3 dc (*UKtr*), 9 dc
(*UKtr*) in next dc (*UKtr*), skip 3 dc (*UKtr*)]**, rep from
** to ** three more times, join with a sl st to beg of
round. Fasten off and work in all the ends.

Vase cover

1 Make three motifs, either in the same or different
colours. Sew them together in a strip.

2 Working along one short end, rejoin the yarn and
work 15 sc (*UKdc*) all along the edge.

3 Turn and work a further two rows of sc (*UKdc*).
Fasten off.

4 Work along the other short end in the same way, but
on the second row work a buttonhole at either end as
follows: work 2 sc (*UKdc*), 3 ch, skip 1 sc (*UKdc*), work
in dc (*UKtr*) to last 3 sc (*UKdc*), 3 ch, skip 1 sc (*UKdc*),
1 sc (*UKdc*) in each of last 2 sc (*UKdc*). Fasten off.

5 Sew in the ends and attach buttons to correspond
with the buttonholes.

*Use this pretty vase cover to decorate
candle holders, flower holders and
drinking glasses.*

BAKER BOY BEANIE

Materials:
1 ball of super bulky (super chunky) merino yarn in lichen green; 100g/87yd/80m

Tools:
Size 10mm (US N/15) crochet hook
Stitch marker (optional)

Size:
Head circumference 21¼–23in (54–58cm)

Gauge (tension) sample
7.5 rose double (*UKtreble*) shells and 5.5 rounds using a 10mm (US N/15) crochet hook = 4 x 4in (10 x 10cm). Change your hook if necessary to obtain the correct gauge (tension).

Special stitch
The hat is worked in spiral rounds of rose double (*UKtreble*) shell. The stitch is not difficult – it begins like double crochet (*UKtreble crochet*) but is finished slightly differently:

Rose double (*UKtreble*) shell (rds/*UKrts*): yrh, insert the hook into the st, yrh, draw through 2 loops (2 loops remaining on hook), yrh, draw through the 2 rem loops. (NB: The design is formed only in the RS rows or rounds.)

Instructions:
Start the cap at the crown and work down to the bottom edge in spiral rounds using rds (*UKrts*).

Begin with 2 ch.

Round 1: Crochet 6 rds (*UKrts*) into the 2nd ch from the hook (see the crochet stitches guide on the book flaps). Mark the start of the round with a contrasting yarn or crochet stitch marker.

Round 2: Work 2 rds (*UKrts*) into each st around (12 sts).

Round 3: Rep round 2 (24 sts).

Round 4: Work * 1 rds (*UKrts*) then work 2 rds (*UKrts*) into the next st * , rep from * to * around (36 sts).

Round 5: Work * 1 rds (*UKrts*) into each of the next 2 sts then work 2 rds (*UKrts*) into the next st * , rep from * to * around (48 sts).

Rounds 6–10: Work 1 rds (*UKrts*) into each st around (48 sts).

Round 11: Work sc2tog (*UKdc2tog*) in every st around (24 sts).

Round 12: Working into the back loop of each st only, work sc (*UKdc*) in every st around then join into a round with a sl st. Cut the yarn.

For the peak (visor) work over 5 rows, as follows. After the 6th st along from the centre back, join in your yarn with a sl st and crochet over the next 12 sts as follows:

Row 1: 1 ch, working into the back loop of each st only, sc (*UKdc*) into each of the next 12 sts.

Rows 2–4: Work back and forth in sc (*UKdc*), working into the back loops only as before (12 sts).

Row 5: Still working in the back loops only, work 1 ch, skip the 1st st, sc (*UKdc*) into each of the next 9 sts, skip the next st, then sc (*UKdc*) into the final st. This rounds off the front.

Making up
Work around the whole peak (visor) in sl st, working 5 sl sts along the RS edge, 10 sl sts along the front and then 5 sl sts on the left edge.

Tip
If you do not like peaked caps, simply leave out the last five rows and wear the hat as a cool beret.

GLIMMERING SNOWFLAKE

Materials:

- 1 ball of No. 5 crochet cotton in white (this is sufficient for several snowflakes); 100g/437yd/400m
- 8 pearl beads
- 1 large pearlised snowflake button
- 20in (0.5m) of narrow white ribbon
- White sewing thread

Hook:

Size 2mm (US B/1, UK 14) crochet hook
Sewing needle

Size:

Approx. 3½in (9cm) in diameter

Instructions:

Make 2 motifs

Using white crochet cotton, make 8 ch then join with sl st into a ring.

Round 1: 7 ch to count as 1 dtr (*UKtrtr*) and 2 ch, *1 dtr (*UKtrtr*) 2 ch into the ring,* repeat from * to * fourteen times more, 2 ch, then join with a sl st into 5th ch of starting ch (16 x 2-ch sps).

Round 2: 2 ch, 2 sc (*UKdc*) into first 2ch sp, *3 sc (*UKdc*) into next 2ch sp,* repeat all around and join with a sl st to beg (48 sts).

Round 3: 8 ch, for first sc (*UKdc*) and 7 ch loop, 1 sc (*UKdc*) into 3rd sc (*UKdc*), *5 ch, skip 2 sc (*UKdc*), 1 sc (*UKdc*) into next sc (*UKdc*), 7 ch, skip 2 sc (*UKdc*), 1 sc (*UKdc*) into next sc (*UKdc*),* repeat from * to * all around, ending last repeat 5 ch, join with sl st to beg. There should be eight 7-ch loops and eight 5-ch loops.

Round 4: sl st into first 7 ch loop, into loop work 3 ch, 4 dc (*UKtr*), 4 ch, sl st into 3rd ch from hook (1 picot made), 1 ch, 5 dc (*UKtr*) into loop, *1 sc (*UKdc*) into next 5-ch loop, [5 dc (*UKtr*), 4 ch, sl st into 3rd ch from hook (1 picot made), 5 dc (*UKtr*)] all into next 7 ch loop,* repeat from * to * all around, ending last rep 1 sc (*UKdc*) into last 5-ch sp, join with a sl st to beg of round. Fasten off.

Making up

Place the two snowflakes back to back and sew them together neatly, matching the points as you do so. Sew the large snowflake button to the centre of the snowflake and then sew a small pearl to the centre of each point, using the photograph as a guide.

Thread the ribbon through the top of one point to make a hanging loop. Decide how long you want the ribbon loop to be and trim the ribbon as necessary. Either tie the ends of the ribbon together in a knot or stitch them to form a loop.

Tip

To give the snowflake a firmer texture, spray fabric stiffener on to it before attaching the button and beads.

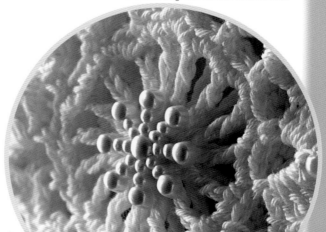

TUDOR ROSE

Materials:

Small amounts of No. 3 crochet
cotton in white, red and lime green;
100g/306yd/280m

Selection of small yellow beads

1 large pearl-shaped bead (pale yellow)

Sewing thread

Tools:

Size 3mm (US D, UK 10) crochet hook

Sewing needle

Instructions:

White flower

For the flower centre, use white
crochet cotton and make 4 ch, join
with sl st into a ring.

Round 1: *3 ch, 3 tr (UKdtr), 3 ch, sl
st into ring*, repeat from * to * four
more times, making 5 petals in total.
Fasten off.

Red flower

Using red yarn for the back of the
flower, make 6 ch, join with sl st
into a ring.

Round 1: *4 ch, 5 dtr (UKttr), 4 ch, sl
st into ring*, repeat from * to * four
more times, making 5 petals in total.
Fasten off.

Leaves

Using green for the leaves, make 8
ch, join with sl st into a ring.

Round 1: *7 ch, skip 1 ch, sc (UKdc)
into next ch, 2 dc (UKtr), 3 tr UKdtr),
sl st into ring*, repeat from * to *
three more times.

Round 2: 7 ch, skip 1 ch, sl st into
next ch, sc (UKdc) into next ch, 2 dc
(UKtr), 2 dtr (UKttr), sl st into base
of first leaf. Fasten off.

Making up

Lay the red flower on the leaves so
that the leaves are visible between
each petal. Sew together.

Lay the white flower on the red
flower so that the red petals lie
between the white petals. Sew
together invisibly.

Sew the large pearl-shaped bead
into the centre of the white flower,
and sew the smaller yellow beads
around it.

BETSY BIRTHDAY BEAR

Instructions:

Make the bear following the instructions on page 37, using light beige for the head, body, arms and legs and mid-brown for the muzzle and ears.

Dress skirt

Round 1: using deep pink yarn, make 30 ch, join with a sl st to beg of row, making sure you do not twist the chain.

Round 2: 1 ch, 1 sc (UKdc) in each ch to end, joining as before.

Round 3: *3 ch, skip 1 sc (UKdc), 1 sc (UKdc) in next sc (UKdc)*, rep from * to * all round, join in 3 ch sp at beg of round.

Round 4: *3 ch, 1 sc (UKdc) in next 3-ch loop*, rep from * to * all round, joining as before.

Round 5: work as row 4.

Round 6: 3 ch, 4 dc (UKtr) in same loop as join, 5 dc (UKtr) in each following 3 ch loop, join with a sl st to top of 3 ch at beg of row. Fasten off.

Fold skirt in half with join at centre back.

Dress bodice

Row 1: working along starting ch, skip first 10 ch, join yarn into next ch, 1 sc (UKdc) in each of next 10 ch, turn.

Row 2: 1 ch, 1 sc (UKdc) in each sc (UKdc) to end, working last sc (UKdc) in place where yarn was joined in, turn.

Rows 3 and 4: sc (UKdc). Fasten off.

Crocheted flower for hat

Round 1: using deep pink yarn, make 4 ch, join in a circle with a sl st.

Round 2: *4 ch, 1 sc (UKdc) in circle*, rep from * to * five times, join with a sl st to beg of row. Fasten off.

Making up

Work in the ends on all the pieces. Make a chain long enough to reach from each corner of the bodice and around the bear's neck. Sew the chain to one corner of the bodice. Slip the dress on to the bear and secure the chain on the other side of the bodice. Sew a deep pink ribbon rose to the centre front of the dress. Thread the crystal beads on to a double length of strong thread to make the necklace. Tie the cotton firmly at the back of the bear's neck and secure. To make the hat, cut a small circle of pink net slightly bigger than the crocheted flower. Gather the circle slightly in the centre. Place the flower on top of the net, take three ribbon roses and place these in the centre of the flower. Now stitch through the roses, flower and net to hold them all together. Sew the hat to the top of the bear's head.

EARRINGS AND PENDANT

Materials:

Small amount of No. 3 crochet cotton in pink; 100g/306yd/280m

Tools:

Size 2.5mm (US B/1, UK 13) crochet hook

2 x jewellery pliers

Notions:

3 x heart-shaped silver hoops

2 x ear wires

3 x jump rings

Chain with clasp

Instructions (make 3):

Attach yarn to heart-shaped hoop, ch 1 and sc (*UKdc*) all around, keeping sts as neat as possible. Make sure you have worked enough sts to conceal the silver heart and sl st into initial ch. Fasten off and weave in loose ends.

Making up

For all three hearts, attach one jump ring to the centre stitch between the heart lobes. Attach an earwire to two of the jump rings to complete the earrings. For the remaining heart, thread the chain through the jump ring to complete the pendant.

PRIMROSE

Materials:
Small amounts of No. 3 crochet cotton in pale green, (A), yellow (B), pale yellow (C), purple (D) and lilac (E); 100g/306yd/280m

Hook:
Size 2.5mm (US B/1, UK 13) crochet hook

Size:
Approx. 4in (10cm) from corner to opposite side

Note

The primrose has five petals, each of which is made up of two half-petals joined into a heart shape.

Instructions:

Using yarn A, ch 4 and join with sl st to first ch to form a ring.

Round 1: 1 ch, 10 sc (UKdc) in ring, sl st to first ch (10 sts). Fasten off.

Round 2: Attach yarn B to any st, 1 ch, 1 sc (UKdc) in same st, 2 sc (UKdc) in each st around, sl st to initial ch. Fasten off (20 sts).

Round 3: Attach yarn C to any st, 4 ch, [1 tr (UKdtr), 1 hdc (UKhtr)] in same st, sl st to next st*, [sl st to next st, 4 ch, 1 tr (UKdtr), 1 hdc (UKhtr)] in same st, sl st to next st, rep from * eight times to end. Fasten off (10 half-petals).

Round 4: Working behind the petals, attach D to base of middle st of any half-petal, 4 ch, *skip one half-petal, attach to base of middle st in next half-petal, 4 ch, rep from *

three times, sl st to where you joined yarn.

Round 5: 4 ch, 1 dc (UKtr) and 1 ch), in next loop work *[3 dc (UKtr), 2 ch, 3 dc (UKtr), 1 ch], rep from * three times, in last loop work [3 dc (UKtr), 2 ch, 2 dc (UKtr)], sl st to third ch of initial 4-ch.

Round 6: sl st into next 1-ch sp, and work [3 ch, 2 dc (UKtr), 1 ch] in same sp, in corner sp work [3 dc (UKtr), 2 ch, 3 dc (UKtr), 1 ch], in 1-ch sps work [3 dc (UKtr), 1 ch]; continue to last corner, then sl st into third ch of initial 3-ch. Fasten off.

Round 7: Attach E into any 1-ch sp, [3 ch, 2 dc (UKtr), 1 ch] in same sp, in corner sp work [3 dc (UKtr), 2 ch, 3 dc (UKtr), 1 ch], in 1-ch sps work [3 dc (UKtr), 1 ch], sl st to third ch of initial 3-ch.

Making up

Fasten off and weave in all loose ends. Block to achieve correct pentagonal shape and pin petals out to dry flat.

The motifs for this lavender bag (opposite) were worked using small amounts of apple (A), clementine (B), primrose (C) and hyacinth (D) Stylecraft Lullaby DK acrylic yarn (50g ball/147yd/135m).

Make two motifs. Block if desired. Use one as a template and cut out two pieces of cotton fabric that are slightly larger than the motif to allow for the seam. Pin them together with RS facing and sew up the seam, leaving one side open. Clip slightly into the corners so you can push them out properly, turn through, then fill with lavender in the centre and toy stuffing round the edges. Sew up the remaining side with white thread, making the stitches as invisible as you can. Holding the two motifs with the WS together and using yarn D, work sc (UKdc) through both motifs round four sides, making 3 sts in each corner. Insert the fabric pad, then crochet the fifth side closed, but when you reach the last hexagon point work 20 ch, sl st in second ch from hook, then sl st in each st to end. Fasten off, attach the end to the other side of the point and weave in loose ends.

FREYA PURSE

Materials:

1 ball of light worsted (DK/8-ply) yarn
in purple (A); 50g/142yd/130m

1 ball of lace weight (2-ply) yarn in light
purple (B); 25g/229yd/210m

Hook:

Size 4mm (US G/6, UK 8) crochet hook

Notions:

1 large button

7in (18cm) zip

Size:

Approx. 5½in (14cm) in diameter

Instructions (make 2):

With yarn A and 4mm (US G/6, UK 8) crochet hook,
make an adjustable ring (see page 21) and work 10 dc
(UKtr) into ring, join with sl st to first st (10 sts).

Round 1: 3 ch (counts as 1 dc (UKtr)), *2 dc (UKtr) in
next st, rep from * to end, 1 dc (UKtr) in base of beg ch,
sl st to third of 3-ch at beg of round (20 sts).

Round 2: As round 1 (40 sts).

Round 3: 3 ch (counts as 1 dc (UKtr)), [2 dc (UKtr) in
next st, 1 dc (UKtr) in next st] eight times, [1 dc (UKtr) in
next st, 2 dc (UKtr) in next st, 1 dc (UKtr) in next st] four
times, [2 dc (UKtr) in next st, 1 dc (UKtr) in next st] five
times, 2 dc (UKtr) in next st, sl st to third of ch-3 at beg
of round (58 sts).

Round 4: 3 ch (counts as 1 dc (UKtr)), *1 dc (UKtr) in
next 2 sts, 2 dc (UKtr) in next st, rep from * to last st,
1 dc (UKtr) in last st, sl st to third of 3-ch at beg of round
(77 sts).

Round 5: 3 ch (counts as 1 dc (UKtr)), 1 dc (UKtr) in each
st to end, sl st to third of ch-3 at beg of round.

Flower

With yarn B and 4mm (US G/6, UK 8) crochet hook,
make 162 ch.

Row 1: Skip 7 ch (counts as 1 dc (UKtr) and 4 ch), 1 dc
(UKtr) in next ch, *ch 4, 1 dc (UKtr) in next ch, rep from
* to end.

Row 2: *[1 dc, 4 dc (UKtr)] into next 4-ch sp, rep from *
until all spaces have been worked.

Fasten off yarn.

Making up

Press front and back pieces lightly with an iron. Wind
the flower in a spiral, securing it to the front of the
purse as you wind. Attach the button to the centre of
the flower. Join the front and back pieces together
leaving a 7in (18cm) gap. Weave in all loose ends and
then sew the zip into the gap.

DAFFODIL SQUARE

Materials:

Small amounts of No. 3 crochet cotton in blue (A), white (B), claret (C) and teal (D); 100g/306yd/280m

Hook:

Size 3mm (US D, UK 10) crochet hook

Size:

3in (7.5cm) diameter

Instructions:

Using A, 8 ch, join with a sl st into a circle.

Round 1: 1 ch, work 16 sc (UKdc) into ring, join as before. Fasten off yarn A.

Round 2: using B, 3 ch, 2 dc (UKtr) into same st, leaving last loop of each dc (UKtr) on hook, yrh and draw yarn through all loops on hook, *2 ch, skip 1 sc (UKdc), 3 dc (UKtr) into next sc (UKdc) leaving last loop of each st on hook, yrh, draw yarn through all loops*, rep from * to * all round, ending last rep with 2 ch, skip 1 sc (UKdc), sl st to top of 3 ch at beg of round. Fasten off yarn B.

Round 3: using C, sl st into first 2 ch sp, 3 ch, 3 dc (UKtr) into same sp, *3 ch, 4 dc (UKtr) into next 2 ch sp*, rep from * to * all round, ending last rep with 3 ch, join with a sl st to top of 3 ch at beg of round. Fasten off yarn C.

Round 4: sl st to first 3 ch sp. Using D, [3 ch, 4 dc (UKtr), 2 ch, 5 dc (UKtr)] into same sp, *4 dc (UKtr) into next sp, [5 dc (UKtr), 2 ch, 5 dc (UKtr)] into next sp*, rep from * to * all round, sl st to top of 3 ch at beg of round. Fasten off and work in all the ends.

Materials:

1 ball of super bulky (super chunky) novelty fluffy wool yarn in toffee brown; 50g/77yd/70m

1 ball of bulky (chunky) wool yarn in dark brown; 50g/90yd/80m

Hook:

Size 5mm (US H/8, UK 6) and 8mm (US L/11) crochet hooks

Size:

Head circumference 21¼–23in (54–58cm)

Gauge (tension) sample

9 sts and 9 rounds of sc (*UKdc*) using the 8mm (US L/11) hook and super bulky (super chunky) novelty fluffy yarn = 4 x 4in (10 x 10cm). Change your hook if necessary to obtain the correct gauge (tension).

Working in spiral rounds

Work sc (*UKdc*) in rounds like spirals, without joining the last stitch of the round to the first stitch in the usual way. Mark the start of the row with a contrasting thread (see page 21).

NB: Crochet the sc (*UKdc*) loosely and before each insertion of the hook, slightly open the next st with the left thumb and index finger to make the fluffy stitches more visible.

Working tr (*UKdtr*)

The flower's petals are worked in treble crochet (*UK double treble*). This long stitch is worked as follows:

Tr (*UKdtr*): yrh twice, insert the hook into the st, yrh and draw through 1 loop (4 loops on hook), yrh and draw through 2 loops (3 loops on hook), yrh and draw through 2 loops (2 loops on hook), yrh and draw through remaining 2 loops.

FIBRE FUN HAT

Instructions:

Start the beanie at the crown and work down to the bottom edge in spiral rounds of sc (*UKdc*).

Begin with 2 ch in the super bulky (super chunky) yarn using the 8mm (US L/11) crochet hook.

Round 1: Work 6 sc (*UKdc*) into the 2nd ch from the hook. Mark the start of the round with a contrasting yarn.

Round 2: Work 2 sc (*UKdc*) into every st around (12 sts).

Round 3: Work * 1 sc (*UKdc*) then work 2 sc (*UKdc*) into the next st *, rep from * to * around (18 sts).

Round 4: Work * sc (*UKdc*) into each of next 2 sts then 2 sc (*UKdc*) into next st *, rep from * to * around (24 sts).

Round 5: Work * sc (*UKdc*) into each of next 3 sts then 2 sc (*UKdc*) into next st *, rep from * to * around (30 sts).

Round 6: Work * sc (*UKdc*) into each of next 4 sts then 2 sc (*UKdc*) into next st *, rep from * to * around (36 sts).

Round 7: Work * sc (*UKdc*) into each of next 5 sts then 2 sc (*UKdc*) into next st *, rep from * to * around (42 st).

Round 8: Work * sc (*UKdc*) into each of next 6 sts then 2 sc (*UKdc*) into next st *, rep from * to * around (48 sts).

Round 9: Work * sc (*UKdc*) into each of next 7 sts then 2 sc (*UKdc*) into next st *, rep from * to * around (54 sts).

Rounds 10–20: Work sc (*UKdc*) into every st around (54 sts).

Rounds 21–26 (hat band): Change to the 5mm (US H/8, UK 6) crochet hook and the chunky (bulky) yarn and continue in spiral rounds. This yarn and hook change will automatically make the edge narrower. Finish the final round with a sl st into the 1st st of the round.

Crochet flowers

Using bulky (chunky) yarn and the 5mm (US H/8, UK 6) crochet hook, ch 5 and join into a ring with a sl st.

Round 1: 1 ch, work 16 sc (*UKdc*) into the ring then join into a round with a sl st (16 sts).

Round 2: Crochet 1 petal into every 2nd st of the previous round by working 1 sc (*UKdc*), 4 ch, 3 tr (*UKdtr*), 4 ch, 1 sc (*UKdc*) all into the same st. Work 8 petals in the round. Close the round with a sl st.

Attach the flower to the side of the hat, using the photograph as a guide.

CHRISTMAS STOCKING

Materials:

- 1 ball of No. 3 crochet cotton in red and a small amount in white; 100g/306yd/280m
- 4 snowflake buttons (8 if you wish to embellish both sides)
- Silver ribbon bow
- 20in (0.5m) of narrow silver ribbon
- Sewing thread to match the buttons and ribbon

Tools:

- Size 2mm (US B/1, UK 14) crochet hook
- Sewing needle

Size:

Approx. 4in (10cm) high

Instructions:

Using white crochet cotton, make 29 ch.
Row 1: 1 sc (*UKdc*) into 2nd ch from hook, 1 sc (*UKdc*) into each ch to end; turn (28 sts).
Rows 2–3: work 1 sc (*UKdc*) into each sc (*UKdc*) to end.
Row 4: join in red. *Insert hook into first sc (*UKdc*) and pull yarn through, then insert hook into corresponding sc (*UKdc*) 2 rows below, draw up loop and work as normal sc (*UKdc*),* repeat to end.
Row 5: using red, work 1 row in sc (*UKdc*).
Row 6: using white, work 1 row in sc (*UKdc*).
Row 7: using white, repeat row 4.
Row 8: using white, work 1 row in sc (*UKdc*).
Rows 9–20: using red, work each st in sc (*UKdc*).

Now create the top of the foot:
Row 1: work in sc (*UKdc*) across 18 sts, turn.
Row 2: work in sc (*UKdc*) across 8 sts, turn.
Rows 3–10: work in sc (*UKdc*) on these 8 sts.
Fasten off yarn.

Foot

Rejoin yarn and work 10 sc (*UKdc*) along the right side of the top of the foot, 8 sc (*UKdc*) across the toe, and 10 sc (*UKdc*) down the left side of top of the foot then finally

work across the remaining 10 sc (*UKdc*) of the foot (48 sts), turn.
Rows 1–6: work in sc (*UKdc*) across all sts.
Row 7: sc (*UKdc*) 2 tog, sc (*UKdc*) 20, sc (*UKdc*) 2 tog twice, sc (*UKdc*) 20, sc (*UKdc*) 2 tog.
Row 8: sc (*UKdc*) 2 tog, sc (*UKdc*) 18, sc (*UKdc*) 2 tog twice, sc (*UKdc*) 18, sc (*UKdc*) 2 tog.
Row 9: sc (*UKdc*) 2 tog, sc (*UKdc*) 16, sc (*UKdc*) 2 tog twice, sc (*UKdc*) 16, sc (*UKdc*) 2 tog.
Row 10: sc (*UKdc*) 2 tog, sc (*UKdc*) 14, sc (*UKdc*) 2 tog twice, sc (*UKdc*) 14, sc (*UKdc*) 2 tog.
Row 11: sc (*UKdc*) 2 tog, work in sc (*UKdc*) to last 2 sts, sc (*UKdc*) 2 tog; fasten off.

Making up

Weave in the loose yarn ends and sew the foot and back seam of the stocking. Attach the snowflake buttons and the ribbon bow, using the photograph as a guide. Fold the silver ribbon in half to make a hanging loop, trimming it to the required length, and attach it to the stocking.

HIBISCUS

Instructions:

With purple crochet cotton, make 8 ch, sc (*UKdc*) into 3rd ch, sc (*UKdc*) to end, turn (6 sts).

Row 1: 1 ch, skip 1 ch, sc (*UKdc*) into next 6 ch, turn.

Row 2: 1 ch, sc (*UKdc*) into next 5 sc (*UKdc*), 2 sc (*UKdc*) into last sc (*UKdc*), turn.

Row 3: 1 ch, sc (*UKdc*) into next 6 sc (*UKdc*), 2 sc (*UKdc*) into last sc (*UKdc*), turn.

Row 4: 1 ch, sc (*UKdc*) into next 7 sc (*UKdc*), 2 sc (*UKdc*) into last sc (*UKdc*), turn.

Row 5: 1 ch, sc (*UKdc*) into next 8 sc (*UKdc*), 2 sc (*UKdc*) into last sc (*UKdc*), turn.

Row 6: 1 ch, sc (*UKdc*) into next 9 sc (*UKdc*), 2 sc (*UKdc*) into last sc (*UKdc*), turn.

Row 7: 1 ch, sc (*UKdc*) into next 10 sc (*UKdc*), 2 sc (*UKdc*) into last sc (*UKdc*), turn.

Row 8: 1 ch, skip 1 sc (*UKdc*), sc (*UKdc*) into next 11 sc (*UKdc*), turn.

Rows 9 and 10: repeat row 8 twice.

Row 11: 1 ch, skip 2 sc (*UKdc*), 7 sc (*UKdc*), skip 2 sc (*UKdc*), ss into last sc (*UKdc*).

Materials:

Small amounts of No. 3 crochet cotton in purple and orange; 100g/306yd/280m

1 small white bead

15 larger orange beads

Sewing thread

Tools:

Size 3mm (US D, UK 10) crochet hook

Sewing needle

85

Row 12: ss, 1 sc (*UKdc*), 2 hdc (*UKhtr*) into same sc (*UKdc*), 1 ch, ss into next sc (*UKdc*), ss into next sc (*UKdc*), 1 ch, 2 hdc (*UKhtr*) into next sc (*UKdc*), 1 sc (*UKdc*) into next sc (*UKdc*), ss into next sc (*UKdc*).

Fasten off.

Repeat all the above instructions, making 5 petals in total.

For the flower centre, thread the orange beads on to the orange crochet cotton, finishing with the white bead. Make a knot at one end.

Push the white bead up to the knot and ch st around it. Make 1 ch then ch st around an orange bead. Continue to ch st around the beads in the order in which they are threaded. If the flower centre is too loose, wrap the remaining crochet cotton around the beads to make it stable.

Layer the petals so that they overlap slightly leaving a ½in (1cm) hole in the centre. Sew gathering stitches along the bottom edges of all the petals. Draw them together slightly. Place the wider end of the orange-beaded flower centre through this hole and sew it in place securely.

This exotic flower works well in bright, tropical colours. Use it to brighten up your summer clothes, bags and accessories.

KATIE WEDDING BEAR

Materials:

1 ball of No. 5 crochet cotton in cream
   and small amounts in mid-brown;
   100g/437yd/400m

Black floss for embroidering features

Toy stuffing

Piece of cream net for veil, 2 x 3¼in
   (5 x 8cm)

7 small yellow and mauve paper roses

12 small white beads for collar

Sewing threads to match crochet cotton

Tools:

Size 2.5mm (US B/1, UK 13)

Sewing needle

Instructions:

Make the bear following the instructions on page 37, using cream for the head, body, arms and legs and mid-brown for the muzzle and ears.

Skirt

Round 1: using cream, make 30 ch, join with a sl st to beg of round, making sure you do not twist the chain.

Round 2 (RS): 1 ch, 1 sc (UKdc) in each ch to end, joining as before.

Round 3: 4 ch, skip 2 sc (UKdc), 1 sc (UKdc) in next sc (UKdc), *2 ch, skip 2 ch, 1 sc (UKdc) in next sc (UKdc)*, rep from * to * all round ending last rep, 2 ch, skip 2 ch, sl st in 2nd of 4 ch at beg of round.

Round 4: sl st in first ch sp, 3 ch, [1 dc (UKtr), 2 ch, 2 dc (UKtr)] in same sp, *[2 dc (UKtr), 2 ch, 2 dc (UKtr)] in next sp*, rep from * to * all round, join in top of 3 ch at beg of round.

Rounds 5 and 6: rep round 4.

Turn, then work edging from WS:

1 dc (UKtr) in next st, sl st in next st, rep from * to * all round, working in all sts and sps, join with a sl st to beg of round. Fasten off.

Crocheted flower for bouquet

Round 1: using cream yarn, make 8 ch and join in ring with a sl st.

Round 2: *4 ch, 1 sc (UKdc) in ring*, rep from * to * five times, join with a sl st.

Round 3: *[1 sc (UKdc), 1 dc (UKtr), 1 sc (UKdc)] in next 4 ch loop, sl st in next sc (UKdc)*, rep from * to * all round and join with a sl st to beg of row. Fasten off.

Crocheted flower for headdress

Round 1: using cream yarn, make 4 ch and join in a circle with a sl st.

Round 2: *4 ch, 1 sc (UKdc) in circle*, rep from * to * five times, join with a sl st to beg of row. Fasten off.

Collar

Row 1: using cream yarn, make 24 ch, 1 sc (UKdc) in 2nd ch from hook, 1 sc (UKdc) in each ch to end, turn.

Row 2: 1 ch, *sl st in next sc (UKdc), 1 dc (UKtr) in next sc (UKdc)*, rep from * to * along row. Fasten off.

Making up

For the headdress, use a needle and matching thread to gather the net across one short edge. Push two paper roses through the centre of the crocheted flower and twist the wire backs of the flowers together to secure them. Attach the gathered net to the crocheted headdress and arrange it on the bear's head. Secure with a few stitches. Take the collar and sew a tiny white bead to each point on the last row. Place the collar around the bear's neck and secure it at the centre back. For the bouquet, take five paper roses and arrange them in a neat bunch. Twist the wire backs together and thread them through the centre of the crocheted flower. Using a needle and matching thread, stitch the flowers to the crochet. Slip the skirt on to the bear with the join at the centre back and secure with a few stitches. Sew the bear's paws to the bouquet on each side.

HEART BROOCH

Materials:

Small amount of light worsted (DK/8-ply) 100% wool
   yarn in mushroom (A); 50g/142yd/130m

Small amount of lace weight (2-ply) mohair yarn in
   heather (B); 25g/219yd/200m

Small piece of thin pink felt

Pale pink sewing thread

Tools:

4mm (US G/6, UK 8) and 3mm (US D, UK 10)
   crochet hooks

Sewing needle

Notions:

Approx. 50 pale pink seed beads

3 large pale pink pearl beads

Brooch back

Size:

From bottom point to centre top
between lobes 2¾in (7cm)

Instructions:

Using yarn A and 4mm (US G/6, UK 8) hook, make an
adjustable ring (see page 21), ch 3 and work 7 dc (*UKtr*)
in ring, ss into top of 3-ch and pull yarn tail to close the
hole (8 sts).

Round 1: 2 ch, hdc (*UKhtr*) in same st, 2 hdc (*UKhtr*) in
each st around sl st to top of 2 ch (16 sts).

Round 2: 2 ch, 1 hdc (*UKhtr*) in each st around, sl st to
top of 2-ch (16 sts).

Round 3: 1 ch, [1 sc (*UKdc*), 1 hdc (*UKhtr*), 1 dc (*UKtr*),
1 tr (*UKdtr*)] in next st, 4 tr (*UKdtr*) in next st, 3 tr
(*UKdtr*) in next st, 3 dc (*UKtr*) in next st, [1 dc (*UKtr*), 1
hdc (*UKhtr*)] in next st, 2 hdc (*UKhtr*) in next st, [1 hdc
(*UKhtr*), 1 dc (*UKtr*)] in next st; [1 dc (*UKtr*), 1 tr (*UKdtr*),
1 dc (*UKtr*)] in centre bottom st.

This completes the left half of the heart; now continue
round 3 by reversing these sts for the right side:

[1 dc (*UKtr*), 1 hdc (*UKhtr*)] in next st, 2 hdc (*UKhtr*) in
next st, [1 hdc (*UKhtr*), 1 dc (*UKtr*)] in next st, 3 dc (*UKtr*)
in next st, 3tr (*UKdtr*) in next st, 4 tr (*UKdtr*) in next st,
[1 tr (*UKdtr*) in next st, 1 dc (*UKtr*), 1 hdc (*UKhtr*), 1 sc
(*UKdc*)], in next st, 1 ch, sl st to initial ch.

Flower

Using yarn B and 3mm (US D, UK 10) hook, ch 26.

Row 1: sc (*UKdc*) in second ch from hook, sc (*UKdc*) to
end (25 sts).

Row 2: 1 ch, *skip 1 st, 5 dc (*UKtr*) in next st, sl st in
next st, rep from * to last st, sl st into last st.

Fasten off, leaving a long tail of yarn, curve the length of
crochet round into a flower shape (see photograph for
guidance) and secure it with a few stitches. Attach it to
the centre of the heart with the yarn tail and fasten off.
Using the sewing needle and pale pink sewing thread,
attach the pale pink seed beads to the edges of the
petals. Then attach the three large beads to the centre
of the flower.

Making up

Using the sewing needle and thread, attach a
rectangular piece of doubled thin felt to the back of the
brooch using blanket stitch, then sew the brooch back
to the felt.

ROSE

Materials:

Small amounts of No. 3 crochet cotton in red (A)
and dark green (B): 100g/306yd/280m

Hook:

Size 2.5mm (US B/1, UK 13) crochet hook

Size:

Approx. 4¼in (11cm) from corner to
opposite corner

Instructions:

Rose

Using yarn A, ch 70, sc (*UKdc*) in second ch from hook
and in each st to end (69 sts).

Row 1: 1 ch, [sl st in next st, 5 tr (*UKdtr*) in next st, sl
st in next st] six times, [sl st in next st, 5 dc (*UKtr*) in
next st, sl st in next st] six times, [sl st in next st, 5 hdc
(*UKhtr*) in next st, sl st in next st] eleven times. Fasten
off, leaving a long yarn tail. Thread the long yarn tail onto
a tapestry needle and begin to wind the small petals
round in a circle. With the bottom straight edge of the
crochet uppermost, make small stitches to secure the
petals in place as you curl them round. Check that the
rose is forming to your satisfaction as you go. Keep
winding the petals round, securing them with small
stitches on the reverse.

*This pretty motif would make a lovely cushion or blanket
if made up using a range of complementary colours for
the flowers.*

Edging

Round 1: Using yarn B, join to centre back of the rose
about ½in (1cm) away from the middle. Identify three
more points that will form a square, equidistant from
the centre of the rose back, 3 ch, sl st to second point, 3
ch, sl st to third point, 3 ch, sl st to fourth point, 3 ch, sl
st back to first point (four 3-ch loops forming a square).

Round 2: sl st to first loop, work [3 ch, 2 dc (*UKtr*), 1 ch,
3 dc (*UKtr*), 2 ch] in same loop, *in next loop work [3 dc
(*UKtr*), 1 ch, 3 dc (*UKtr*), 2 ch] rep from * twice, sl st to
third ch of initial 3-ch.

Round 3: sl st to next 1-ch sp, work [3 ch, 2 dc (*UKtr*), 1
ch] in same sp; *in corner sp work [3 dc (*UKtr*), 2 ch, 3
dc (*UKtr*), 1 ch], in next space work [3 dc (*UKtr*), 1 ch],
rep from * twice, in next sp work [3 dc (*UKtr*), 2 ch, 3
dc (*UKtr*), 1 ch], sl st to third ch of initial 3-ch.

Round 4: sl st to next 1-ch sp, work [3 ch, 2 dc (*UKtr*),
1 ch], in same sp; in each corner sp work [3 dc (*UKtr*),
2 ch, 3 dc (*UKtr*), 1 ch]; in each 1-ch sp along straight
edges work [3 dc (*UKtr*), 1 ch], sl st to third ch of
initial 3-ch.

Making up

Fasten off and weave in all loose ends. Block the edging
to achieve a good square shape, but not the rose.

TATE PURSE

Materials:

1 ball each of light worsted (DK/8-ply) yarn in ginger (A), avocado (B), yellow (C) and light brown (D); 50g/191yd/175m

Hook:

3.75mm (US F/5, UK 9) crochet hook

Notions:

1 x magnetic flex frame kiss clasp, approx. 4¾in (12cm)

Size:

Approx. 3½ x 5¼in (9 x 13.5cm)

Instructions:

With yarn A and 3.75mm (US F/5) crochet hook, make 64 ch.

Row 1: Skip 3 ch (counts as 1 dc (*UKtr*)), 2 dc (*UKtr*) in next ch, *skip 3 ch, 1 sc (*UKdc*) in next ch, 3 ch, 1 dc (*UKtr*) in next 3 ch, rep from * to last 4 ch, skip 3 ch, 1 sc (*UKdc*) in last ch. Change to yarn B.

Row 2: 3 ch (counts as 1 dc (*UKtr*)), 2 dc (*UKtr*) in first sc (*UKdc*), *skip 3 dc (*UKtr*), 1 sc (*UKdc*) in first of 3-ch, 3 ch, 3 dc (*UKtr*) in next 2-ch sp, rep from * to last 2 dc (*UKtr*), skip 2 dc (*UKtr*), 1 sc (*UKdc*) in top chain of previous round.

Rep row 2 eleven more times, changing colour on every row to yarn C and D then A, B, C and D again, ending last row with colour A.

Fasten off yarn.

Making up

With WS facing, fold the work in half and turn it around, so that the sides are now at the top. Stitch the magnetic flex frame into place by turning a hem over it at the purse opening, and then sew up the sides. You may wish to line the inside of the purse with a piece of felt.

CAPPUCCINO LACE SQUARE

Instructions:

Using A, make 10 ch, join into a circle with a sl st.

Round 1: 3 ch, work 31 dc (UKtr) into circle, join with a sl st to top of 3 ch at beg of round (32 sts).

Round 2: 1 sc (UKdc) into same sp as join, *7 ch, skip 3 sc (UKdc), 1sc (UKdc) into next sc (UKdc)*, rep from * to * all round, work last sc (UKdc) into same sp as join of previous round. Fasten off yarn A.

Round 3: using B, sl st to 4th ch of first 7 ch sp, 3 ch, 2 dc (UKtr) into same sp but leave last loop of each st on hook, yrh, draw loop through, 3 ch, 3 dc (UKtr) into same st, leaving last loop of each st on hook, yrh and draw through all loops (cluster made), *3 ch into 4th ch of next 7 ch loops, cluster, 3 ch, cluster*, rep from * to * all round, ending last rep with 3 ch, sl st to top of 3 ch at beg of round. Fasten off yarn B.

Round 4: using C, 3 dc (UKtr), 3 ch, 3 dc (UKtr) into first 3 ch sp, *2 ch, 1 sc (UKdc) into next sp, 2 ch, 1 sc (UKdc) into next sp, 2 ch, 1 sc (UKdc) into next sp**, 3 dc (UKtr), 3 ch, 3 dc (UKtr) into next sp*, rep from * to * all round ending last rep at **, sl st to top of 3 ch at beg of round. Fasten off and work in all the ends.

To make the cushion

Make eight squares, four as described in the pattern and four swapping yarns A and B. Work in the ends and join the squares together in 2 rows of 4 squares, alternating the colours as shown.

Join yarn C to any corner and proceed to work around the entire perimeter of the cushion as follows:

Round 1: 3 ch,1 dc (UKtr), 2 ch, 2 dc (UKtr) into same corner sp, now work along the top of each square, working 1 dc (UKtr) into each dc (UKtr) and sc (UKdc) and 2 sc (UKdc) into each sp, to first corner, work 2 dc (UKtr), 3 ch, 2 dc (UKtr) into corner sp, continue in the same way all around the cushion front, joining with a sl st to the top of 3 ch at beg of round.

Materials:

Small amounts of No. 3 crochet cotton in pink (A), cream (B) and green (C); 100g/306yd/280m

For the cushion:

Size 3.75mm (US F/5, UK 9) crochet hook

1 ball each of No. 3 crochet cotton in three colours: A, B and C

Cushion pad, 10 x 17in (25.5 x 43cm)

Gauge (tension) for pattern on back: 17 dc (UKtr) x 9 rows = 4in (10cm)

Hooks:

Size 3mm (US D, UK 10) and 3.75mm (US F/5, UK 9) crochet hooks

Size:

3in (7.5cm) diameter

Round 2: 3 ch, 1 dc (UKtr) into next dc (UKtr), 3 ch, 2 dc (UKtr) into corner sp, continue to work 1 dc (UKtr) into each dc (UKtr) all round the piece, working 2 dc (UKtr), 3 ch, 2 dc (UKtr) into each corner sp, join as before. Fasten off.

Back

Using a 3.75mm (US F/5, UK 9) hook and C, make 44 ch, 1 dc (UKtr) into 3rd ch from hook, 1 dc (UKtr) into each ch to end, turn (42 sts).

Row 1: *3 ch, 1 dc (UKtr) into next dc (UKtr), skip 1 dc (UKtr), 1 dc (UKtr) in next dc (UKtr), 1 dc (UKtr) into skipped st*, rep from * to * all across row, ending 1 dc (UKtr) into each of last 2 dc (UKtr), turn.

Row 2: 3 ch, 1 dc (UKtr) into each dc (UKtr) across row, turn.

These 2 rows form the pattern and are repeated. Continue in pattern until work is the same length as the front. Fasten off.

Work in all loose ends. Join the back of the cushion cover to the front, leaving a gap for the cushion pad. Insert the pad and close up.

Materials:

1 x ball of lace weight (2-ply) mohair blend yarn in pink; 25g/230yd/210m

Hook:

Size 6mm (US J/10, UK 4) crochet hook

Size:

Head circumference 21¼–23in (54–58cm)

Gauge (tension) sample

11 sts and 10 rounds in hdc (*UKhtr*) using lace weight mohair blend yarn = 4 x 4in (10 x 10cm). Change your hook if necessary to obtain the correct gauge (tension).

Working tr (*UK dtr*)

This stitch is used for the flower petals.

Tr (*UK dtr*): yrh twice, insert the hook into the st, yrh and draw through 1 loop (4 loops on hook), yrh and draw through 2 loops (3 loops on hook), yrh and draw through 2 loops (2 loops on hook), yrh and draw through rem 2 loops.

Basic pattern

Crochet spiral rounds of staggered hdc (*UKhtr*), working very loosely. To work staggered hdc (*UKhtr*), instead of putting the hook into the st of the previous round, put it between 2 hdc (*UKhtr*) of the previous round, then work the hdc (*UKhtr*) as normal. This will produce the mesh effect. Mark the start of each round with a contrasting yarn.

Crochet flower

Work 5 ch using double yarn and join into a ring with a sl st. Work 1 ch at the start of the round, then for each petal work * 1 sc (*UKdc*), 3 ch, 3 htr (*UKdtr*), crochet 3 ch into the ring * . Rep from * to * six more times to make 7 petals. Close up the round with a sl st into the 1st ch of the round.

Attach the flower to the side of the finished hat, using the photograph as a guide.

PRETTY IN PINK BEANIE

Instructions:

Start the beanie at the crown and work down to the bottom edge in spiral rounds.

Begin with 2 ch.

Round 1: Work 8 hdc (*UKhtr*) into the 2nd ch from the hook. Mark the start of the round with a contrasting yarn and continue working in spirals of staggered hdc (*UKhtr*).

Round 2: work 2 hdc (*UKhtr*) into each st around (16 sts).

Round 3: Work * 1 hdc (*UKhtr*) then work 2 hdc (*UKhtr*) into the next st * , rep from * to * around (24 sts).

Round 4: Work * 1 hdc (*UKhtr*) into each of the next 2 sts, then 2 hdc (*UKhtr*) into the next st *, rep from * to * around (32 sts).

Round 5: Work * 1 hdc (*UKhtr*) into each of the next 3 sts, then 2 hdc (*UKhtr*) into the next st *, rep from * to * around (40 sts).

Round 6: Work * 1 hdc (*UKhtr*) into each of the next 4 sts, then 2 hdc (*UKhtr*) into the next st *, rep from * to * around (48 sts).

Round 7: Work * 1 hdc (*UKhtr*) into each of the next 5 sts, then 2 hdc (*UKhtr*) into the next st *, rep from * to * around (56 sts).

Round 8: Work * 1 hdc (*UKhtr*) into each of the next 6 sts, then 2 hdc (*UKhtr*) into the next st *, rep from * to * around (64 sts).

Round 9: Work * 1 hdc (*UKhtr*) into each of the next 7 sts, then 2 hdc (*UKhtr*) into the next st *, rep from * to * around (72 sts).

Round 10: Work * 1 hdc (*UKhtr*) into each of the next 8 sts, then 2 hdc (*UKhtr*) into the next st *, rep from * to * around (80 sts).

Round 11: Work * 1 hdc (*UKhtr*) into each of the next 9 sts, then 2 hdc (*UKhtr*) into the next st *, rep from * to * around (88 sts).

Rounds 12–21: work 1 hdc (*UKhtr*) into each st around (88 sts).

Round 22 (hat band): Work spiral rounds of sc (*UKdc*) to create the band, using the yarn double by taking the yarn end from the other end of the ball. Decrease in this round by working sc2tog (*UKdc2tog*) into each st around (44 sts).

Rounds 23–25: Work sc (*UKdc*) into each st around with double yarn. Close round 25 with a sl st into the 1st st of the round. Work these rounds tightly or loosely to obtain the correct fit.

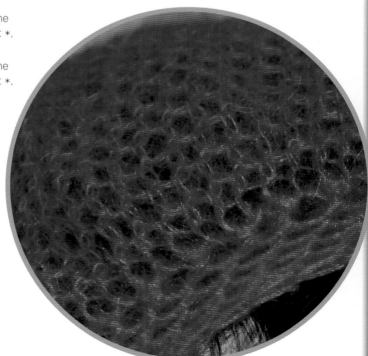

RUDOLF THE REINDEER

Materials:

1 ball each of No. 5 crochet cotton in mid-brown and dark brown; 100g/437yd/400m

Oddment of red metallic yarn

Black embroidery floss or oddment of black crochet cotton

Tiny gold bow and bell embellishment

Small amount of stuffing

Sewing threads to match the yarn

Tools:

Size 2mm (US B/1, UK 14)

Sewing needle

Size:

Approx. 4in (10cm) high to the top of the head

Instructions:

Body

Using mid-brown crochet cotton, make 2 sc (*UKdc*).

Round 1: work 6 sc (*UKdc*) into 2nd ch from hook then join with a sl st to form a tight circle.

Round 2: work 2 sc (*UKdc*) into each st around (12 sts).

Round 3: *1 sc (*UKdc*) into next sc (*UKdc*), 2 sc (*UKdc*) into next sc (*UKdc*),* repeat from * to * all around (18 sts).

Round 4: *1 sc (*UKdc*) into each of next 2 sc (*UKdc*), 2 sc (*UKdc*) into next sc (*UKdc*),* repeat from * to * all around (24 sts).

Round 5: *1 sc (*UKdc*) into each of next 3 sc (*UKdc*), 2 sc (*UKdc*) into next sc (*UKdc*),* repeat from * to * all around (30 sts).

Rounds 6–16: work in sc (*UKdc*) all around.

You will now begin decreasing. Stuff the body as you work.

Round 17: *1 sc (*UKdc*) into each of next 3 sc (*UKdc*), sc (*UKdc*) 2 tog,* repeat from * to * all around.

Round 18: *1 sc (*UKdc*) into each of next 2 sc (*UKdc*), sc (*UKdc*) 2 tog,* repeat from * to * all around.

Round 19: work in sc (*UKdc*) all around.

Round 20: sc (*UKdc*) 2 tog all around. Break yarn. Finish stuffing the body and then run the yarn through the last row of sts, draw up and fasten off.

Head

Using mid-brown crochet cotton, make 2 sc (*UKdc*).

Round 1: work 6 sc (*UKdc*) into 2nd ch from hook then join with a sl st to form a tight circle.

Round 2: work 2 sc (*UKdc*) into each st around (12 sts).

Round 3: *1 sc (*UKdc*) into next sc (*UKdc*), 2 sc (*UKdc*) into next sc (*UKdc*),* repeat from * to * all around (18 sts).

Rounds 4–7: work in sc (*UKdc*) all around.

Round 8: *1 sc (*UKdc*) into each of next 2 sc (*UKdc*), 2 sc (*UKdc*) into next sc (*UKdc*),* repeat from * to * all around then join with a sl st.

Round 9: work in sc (*UKdc*) all around then join with a sl st.

Round 10: *1 sc (*UKdc*) into next sc (*UKdc*), 2 sc (*UKdc*) into next sc (*UKdc*),* repeat from * to * all around then join with a sl st as before.

Rounds 11–15: work 1 sc (*UKdc*) into each sc (*UKdc*) all around then join with a sl st as before.

You will now begin decreasing. Stuff the head as you work.

Round 16: *1 sc (*UKdc*) in each of next 2 sc (*UKdc*), sc (*UKdc*) 2 tog,* repeat from * to * all around then join with a sl st as before.

Round 17: work in sc (*UKdc*) all around then join with a sl st.

Round 18: *1 sc (*UKdc*) into next sc (*UKdc*), sc (*UKdc*) 2 tog,* repeat from * to * all around then join with a sl st.

Round 19: work in sc (*UKdc*) all around then join with a sl st.

Round 20: sc (*UKdc*) 2 tog all around then join with a sl st. Fasten off.

Finish stuffing the head, if needed, then run the yarn through the last row of sts and draw up tight. Fasten off yarn.

Front legs (make 2)

Using mid-brown crochet cotton, make 6 ch.

Row 1: 1 sc (*UKdc*) into 2nd ch from hook, 1 sc (*UKdc*) into each ch to end, turn.

Rows 2–3: work in sc (*UKdc*), increasing 1 sc (*UKdc*) at each end of row.

Work 4 rows in sc (*UKdc*).

Break mid-brown and join in dark brown.

Work 2 rows in sc (*UKdc*).

Next row: work in sc (*UKdc*), increasing 1 sc (*UKdc*) at each end of row.

Next row: work in sc (*UKdc*). Fasten off.

Back legs (make 2)

Using mid-brown crochet cotton, make 10 ch.

Row 1: 1 sc (*UKdc*) into 2nd ch from hook, 1 sc (*UKdc*) into each ch to end, turn.

Row 2: 1 ch, 1 sc (*UKdc*) into each sc (*UKdc*) to end, turn.

Rows 3–4: work in sc (*UKdc*), increasing 1 sc (*UKdc*) at each end of row.

Work 8 rows in sc (*UKdc*).

Change to dark brown and work 4 rows in sc (*UKdc*).

Next row: work in sc (*UKdc*), decreasing 1 sc (*UKdc*) at each end of row.

Next row: repeat previous row. Fasten off.

Large antlers (make 2)

Using dark brown crochet cotton, make 12 ch.

Row 1: 1 sc (*UKdc*) into 2nd ch from hook, 1 sc (*UKdc*) into each ch to end, turn.

Rows 2–4: 1 ch, 1 sc (*UKdc*) into each sc (*UKdc*) to end, turn.

Fasten off.

Small antlers (make 2)

Using dark brown crochet cotton, make 6 ch.

Row 1: 1 sc (*UKdc*) into 2nd ch from hook, 1 sc (*UKdc*) into each ch to end, turn.

Rows 2–4: 1 ch, 1 sc (*UKdc*) into each sc (*UKdc*) to end, turn.

Fasten off.

Ears (make 2)

Using mid-brown crochet cotton, make 2 ch.

Row 1: work 1 sc (*UKdc*) into 2nd ch from hook.

Row 2: 1 ch, 3 sc (*UKdc*) into next sc (*UKdc*), turn.

Rows 3–4: 1 ch, 1 sc (*UKdc*) into each sc (*UKdc*) to end, turn.

Row 5: 1 ch, sc (*UKdc*) 2 tog, 1 sc (*UKdc*) in last sc (*UKdc*), turn.

Row 6: sc (*UKdc*) 2 tog. Fasten off.

Nose

Using red metallic yarn, make 2 ch. Work 14 dc (*UKtr*) into 2nd ch from hook then join with a sl st to first dc (*UKtr*) worked. Fasten off.

Making up

Work in all the ends. Attach the red nose to the head. With black cotton embroider the eyes with French knots and use straight stitches for the mouth. Sew the ears on to each side of the head, using the photograph as a guide. Fold each antler in half lengthways and stitch along the side seam. Sew a short antler on to each long antler at a slight angle, using the photograph as a guide. Now sew the antlers to the head just above the ears. Sew the head on to the body.

Fold the front legs in half lengthways and sew the side seams. Stuff lightly, adding extra at the hoof (dark brown) end to pad them out a little. Oversew a length of cotton through the centre of the hoof end to create the cloven effect. Make up the back legs in the same way. Attach the legs to the body, remembering that Rudolf is sitting down.

FOXGLOVES

Materials:
Small amount of No. 3 crochet cotton in pale pink;
   100g/306yd/280m

Hook:
Size 2.5mm (US B/1, UK 13) crochet hook

Instructions:

With pale pink crochet cotton, make an adjustable ring (see page 21). 2 ch, 9 sc (*UKdc*), pull together, join with a sl st.

Round 1: 2 ch, sc (*UKdc*) into next 9 sc (*UKdc*) join with sl st into 2-ch sp.

Round 2: repeat round 1.

Round 3: 2 ch, 9 hdc (*UKhtr*), sl st into 2 ch.

Round 4: 3 ch, 9 dc (*UKtr*), sl st into 2 ch.

Round 5: 3 ch, 9 dc (*UKtr*), 1 sc (*UKdc*), turn.

Round 6: skip 1 ch, sc (*UKdc*), 2 hdc (*UKhtr*) into same dc (*UKtr*), 1 dc (*UKtr*), 1 tr (*UKdtr*), 3 dtr (*UKttr*) into same dc (*UKtr*), 1 tr (*UKdtr*), 1 dc (*UKtr*), 2 hdc (*UKhtr*) into same dc (*UKtr*), 1 sc (*UKdc*), 1 sl st.

Fasten off and sew in all loose ends.

These dainty foxgloves look gorgeous adorning tablecloths or napkins.

Materials:

1 ball of No. 5 crochet cotton in beige, and
  small amounts in black, brown and cream;
  100g/437yd/400m

Small amount of fingering (4-ply) yarn in
  pale grey

Black floss for embroidering features

Small pearl bead for tie pin

1 yellow paper rose

Narrow satin ribbon in pale grey

Toy stuffing

Sewing threads to match crochet cotton

Tools:

Size 2.5mm (US B/1, UK 13) crochet hook

Sewing needle

ANDREW BRIDEGROOM BEAR

Instructions:

Make the bear following the instructions on page 37, using beige for the head, body, arms and legs and brown for the muzzle and ears.

Top hat crown

Round 1: using grey, make 2 ch, 6 sc (*UKdc*) in 2nd ch, join with a sl st.

Round 2: 2 sc (*UKdc*) in each sc (*UKdc*). Join with a sl st to beg of row.

Round 3: *1 sc (*UKdc*) in next sc (*UKdc*), 2 sc (*UKdc*) in next sc (*UKdc*)*, rep from * to * all round. Join as before. Fasten off.

Top hat side

Row 1: using grey, make 6 ch, 1 sc (*UKdc*) in 2nd ch from hook, 1 sc (*UKdc*) in each ch to end, turn.

Row 2: 1 sc (*UKdc*) into each sc (*UKdc*) to end, turn.

Continue on these 5 sts for a further 22 rows.

Fasten off.

Hat brim

Round 1: using grey, make 27 ch, join in a circle with a sl st, making sure you do not twist the chain.

Round 2: 1 sc (*UKdc*) in each ch all round, join with a sl st to beg of round.

Round 3: 1 sc (*UKdc*) in first sc (*UKdc*), *2 sc (*UKdc*) in next sc (*UKdc*), 1 sc (*UKdc*) in next sc (*UKdc*)*, rep from * to * all round, join as before.

Round 4: sl st in each sc (*UKdc*) all round. Fasten off.

Waistcoat

Row 1: using black, make 30 ch, 1 sc (*UKdc*) in 2nd ch from hook, 1 sc (*UKdc*) in each ch to end.

Rows 2–4: work 3 rows sc (*UKdc*).

Row 5: work across 6 sc (*UKdc*), turn.

Row 6: work to last 2 sc (*UKdc*), sc (*UKdc*) 2 tog.

Row 7: sc (*UKdc*) 2 tog, work to end.

Row 8: work to last 2 sc (*UKdc*), sc (*UKdc*) 2 tog.

Row 9: sc (*UKdc*) 2 tog, work to end (2 sts).

Rows 10 and 11: work 2 rows sc (*UKdc*). Fasten off.

Rejoin yarn, skip 4 sc (*UKdc*), join to next sc (*UKdc*), work 10 sc (*UKdc*), turn and continue on these sts for back.

Work 8 rows sc (*UKdc*). Fasten off.

Next row: skip 4 sc (*UKdc*), rejoin yarn to rem sts and work other front to match, reversing shaping.

Cravat

Row 1: using cream, make 7 ch, 1 sc (*UKdc*) in 2nd ch from hook, 1 sc (*UKdc*) in each ch to end, turn.

Row 2: 1 ch, 1 sc (*UKdc*) in each sc (*UKdc*) to end, turn.

Rep row 2 until piece is 4¾in (12cm) long. Fasten off.

Making up

Work in the ends on all the pieces. Take the side piece of the top hat and join the two short ends together to form a cylinder. Place the crown on to one end of the cylinder and stitch it carefully in place. Slip the brim over the hat, position it carefully and then stitch it in place. Take the ribbon and cut a piece to fit around the hat, leaving a tiny overlap. Stitch it in place. Catch the top hat to the bear's paw with a few stitches. Tie the cravat around the bear's neck, pouch slightly and sew a pearl bead to the centre to represent a tie pin. Sew the shoulder seams on the waistcoat and slip it on to the bear. Arrange the cravat under the waistcoat. Catch the waistcoat together at the front edge with a few stitches and attach a paper rose. Personalise your bear by attaching a suitable button or charm to one of his paws.

SNOWFLAKES

Instructions:

Heart
Round 1: Using yarn A, ch 4, 5 dc (UKtr) in fourth ch from hook, 1 ch, 1 tr (UKdtr), 1 ch, 5 dc (UKtr), 3 ch, sl st in centre (13 sts). Fasten off.

Snowflake points
Round 2: Join yarn B to bottom point of heart with sl st, 5 ch, skip 2 sts and sl st into third st, 5 ch, skip 2 sts and sl st into third st (at top right lobe of heart), 5 ch, sl st into top of 3 ch (at top left lobe of heart), 5 ch, skip 2 sts and sl st into third st, 5 ch and sl st into bottom point of heart.

Round 3 (working into the first 5-ch space): *1 ch, 1 sc (UKdc), 2 hdc (UKhtr), 1 dc (UKtr), 1 ch, sl st into top of dc (UKtr) just worked, 2 hdc (UKhtr), 1 sc (UKdc), sl st into next 5-ch*; rep from * to * into each 5-ch sp, ending with a sl st into initial 1-ch.

Fasten off and weave in all loose ends.

Block as desired.

Materials:
Small amounts of No. 3 crochet cotton in various colours (A), and white (B); 100g/306yd/280m

Hook:
Size 3mm (US D, UK 10) crochet hook

Size:
2³⁄₈in (6cm) at widest point

107

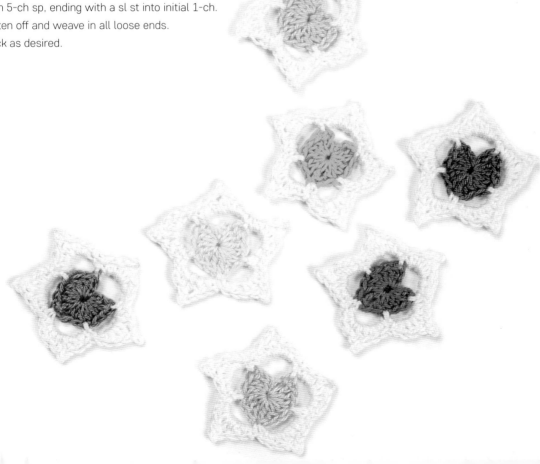

You can either leave the petals to curl naturally, or pin them out for a straighter effect when you block this motif.

NARCISSUS

Materials:
Small amounts of No. 3 crochet cotton in yellow (A), orange (B), mid-green (C) pale green (D) and scarlet (E); 100g/280m/306yd

Tools:
Size 2.5mm (US B/1, UK 13) crochet hook

Size:
Approx. 4¼in (11cm) from corner to opposite corner

Stitch note

The picot stitch is worked as follows: work 2 ch, sl st into second ch from hook.

Instructions:

Using yarn A, ch 4, sl st to first ch to form a ring.

Round 1: 2 ch, work 17 sc (*UKdc*) into ring. Join with a sl st to top of initial ch-2 (18 sts).

Round 2: *sl st into next st, 8 ch, 1 picot, 2 sc (*UKdc*), 2 hdc (*UKhtr*), 3 dc (*UKtr*), skip 1 st, sl st into next st, sl st into next st, rep from * five times (6 petals). Fasten off.

Round 3: Using yarn B, work into the skipped sts from Round 2. Join yarn to any skipped st, 2 ch, 1 sc (*UKdc*) in same st, *in next skipped st, work 2 sc (*UKdc*), rep from * four times, then sl st to initial 2-ch (12 sts).

Round 4: Place st marker in first st, as you will now work in a spiral, 1 sc (*UKdc*) in each st around (12 sts).

Round 5: Move st marker up, work *[1 sc (*UKdc*), 1 picot], rep from * to st marker (the picots will create six little points). Fasten off.

Round 6: Using yarn C, join yarn to st between petals, 3 ch, *sl st to next st between petals, 3 ch, rep from * four times, sl st to first st (six 3-ch loops).

Round 7: sl st to first loop, in first loop work [3 ch, 2 dc (*UKtr*), 1 ch], in next ch-3 sp work [4 dc (*UKtr*), 1 ch] around to end, sl st to first st.

Round 8: sl st to first loop, work [3 ch, 2 dc (*UKtr*), 1 ch, 3 dc (*UKtr*)] in same loop, then in each 1-ch sp work [3 dc (*UKtr*), 1 ch, 3 dc (*UKtr*)] to end. Fasten off.

Round 9: Using yarn D, attach yarn to any 1-ch sp, work [3 ch, 3 dc (*UKtr*)] in same sp, in next and each remaining ch-sp work 4 dc (*UKtr*).

Round 10: 1 ch, work 1 sc (*UKdc*) in each st and each ch-sp around, sl st to beg ch. Fasten off.

To give the impression of stamens, secure yellow, orange and scarlet yarns to the back of the work and make loops in the trumpet, securing again at back of work. Cut through loops and trim stamens to size.

Making up

Fasten off and weave in all loose ends.

Block carefully, shaping the narcissus trumpet with your fingers while the crochet is wet.

Materials:

1 ball each of worsted yarn (light aran) in smoke (A),
cherry red (B) and green (C); 50g/153yd/140m

Hook:

Size 4mm (US G/6, UK 8) crochet hook

Notions:

1 snap fastener

Small amount of toy stuffing

Size:

Approx. 4in (10cm) high and
6in (15cm) at the widest point

CHERRY PURSE

Instructions:

With yarn A and 4mm (US G/6, UK 8) crochet hook, make 18 ch.

Round 1: 2 sc (*UKdc*) in second ch from hook, 1 sc (*UKdc*) in next 15 ch, 4 sc (*UKdc*) in next ch, working on the other side of ch, 1 sc (*UKdc*) in next 15 ch, 2 sc (*UKdc*) in last ch, sl st to first st (38 sts).

Round 2: 1 ch, 2 sc (*UKdc*) in next 2 sts, 1 sc (*UKdc*) in next 15 sts, 2 sc (*UKdc*) in next 4 sts, 1 sc (*UKdc*) in next 15 sts, 2 sc (*UKdc*) in next 2 sts, sl st to first st (46 sts).

Round 3: 1 ch, [1 sc (*UKdc*) in next st, 2 sc (*UKdc*) in next st] twice, 1 sc (*UKdc*) in next 15 sts, [2 sc (*UKdc*) in next st, 1 sc (*UKdc*) in next st] four times, 1 sc (*UKdc*) in next 15 sts, [2 sc (*UKdc*) in next st, 1 sc (*UKdc*) in next st] twice, sl st to first st (54 sts).

Round 4: 1 ch, [1 sc (*UKdc*) in next st, 2 sc (*UKdc*) in next st] three times, 1 sc (*UKdc*) in next 15 sts, [2 sc (*UKdc*) in next st, 1 sc (*UKdc*) in next st] six times, 1 sc (*UKdc*) in next 15 sts, [2 sc (*UKdc*) in next st, 1 sc (*UKdc*) in next st] three times, sl st to first st (66 sts).

Round 5: 1 ch, sc2tog (*UKdc2tog*), 1 sc (*UKdc*) in every st to end, sl st to first st (65 sts).

Rounds 6–8: 1 ch, 1 sc (*UKdc*) in every st to end, sl st to first st.

Round 9: 1 ch, *1 sc (*UKdc*) in next 5 sts, sc2tog (*UKdc2tog*), rep from * to last 2 sts, 1 sc (*UKdc*) in next 2 sts, sl st to first st (56 sts).

Rounds 10–13: 1 ch, 1 sc (*UKdc*) in every st to end, sl st to first st.

Round 14: 1 ch, *1 sc (*UKdc*) in next 4 sts, sc2tog (*UKdc2tog*), rep from * to last 2 sts, 1 sc (*UKdc*) in next 2 sts, sl st to first st (47 sts).

Rounds 15–18: 1 ch, 1 sc (*UKdc*) in every st to end, sl st to first st.

Round 19: 1 ch, sc2tog (*UKdc2tog*), 1 sc (*UKdc*) in next 3 sts, sc2tog (*UKdc2tog*), 1 sc (*UKdc*) in next 11 sts, sc2tog (*UKdc2tog*), [1 sc (*UKdc*) in next 3 sts, sc2tog (*UKdc2tog*)] twice, 1 sc (*UKdc*) in next 11 sts, sc2tog (*UKdc2tog*), 1 sc (*UKdc*) in next 4 sts, sl st to first st (41 sts).

Rounds 20–29: 1 ch, 1 sc (*UKdc*) in every st to end, sl st to first st.

Fasten off yarn.

Cherries (make 2)

With yarn B and 4mm (US G/6, UK 8) crochet hook, make 4 ch, sl st to first ch to form a ring.

Round 1: 1 ch, 6 sc (*UKdc*) into ring, sl st to first st (6 sts).

Round 2: 1 ch, 2 sc (*UKdc*) in every st to end, sl st to first st (12 sts).

Rounds 3 and 4: 1 ch, 1 sc (*UKdc*) in every st to end, sl st to first st.

Round 5: 1 ch, *sc2tog (*UKdc2tog*), rep from * to end, sl st to first st (6 sts).

Fill cherry with toy stuffing.

Round 6: 1 ch, *sc2tog (*UKdc2tog*), rep from * to end, sl st to first st (3 sts).

Fasten off yarn.

Leaf (make 2)

With yarn C and 4mm (US G/6, UK 8) crochet hook, make 8 ch.

Row 1: 1 sc (*UKdc*) into second ch from hook, 1 hdc (*UKhtr*) in next ch, 1 dc (*UKtr*) in next ch, 1 tr (*UKdtr*) in next ch, 1 dc (*UKtr*) in next ch, 1 hdc (*UKhtr*) in next ch, 1 sc (*UKdc*) in next ch.

Fasten off.

Stem (make 2)

With yarn C held double and 4mm (US G/6, UK 8) crochet hook, make 5 ch, fasten off yarn.

Attach the stems to the cherries and leaves.

Making up

Weave in all loose ends. Fold the top of the purse over (around 1in (2.5cm)) to create a cuff.

Attach the leaves to the cuff, using the photograph as a guide. Sew the snap fastener to the inside of the purse at the centre top.

SCALLOPED CIRCLE

Materials:

Small amounts of No. 3 crochet cotton
in three colours: peach (A), cream (B)
and beige (C); 100g/306yd/280m

Hook:

Size 3mm (US D, UK 10)
crochet hook

Size:

3½in (9cm) diameter

Instructions:

Using A, make 8 ch, join into a circle with a
sl st.

Round 1: 3 ch [counts as first dc (UKtr)], work
2 dc (UKtr) into ring, leaving the last loop of
each dc (UKtr) on the hook, now draw the yarn
through all loops on the hook, *2 ch, work 3
dc (UKtr) into ring, leaving last loop of each dc
(UKtr) on the hook, yrh, draw the yarn through
all 3 loops*, rep from * to * seven more times,
2 ch, join with a sl st to beg of round (9 clusters
in total). Fasten off yarn A.

Round 2: using B, *2 ch, 1 sc (UKdc) into next
sp, 2 ch, 1sc (UKdc) into top of cluster*, rep
from * to * all round, 2 ch, join with a sl st to
beg of round (18 x 2 ch sp).

Round 3: 6 ch [counts as first dc (UKtr) and 3
ch], 1 dc (UKtr) into next 2 ch sp, *3 ch, 1 dc
(UKtr) into next 2 ch sp*, rep from * to * all
round, 3 ch, join with a sl st to 3rd ch at beg of
round. Fasten off yarn B.

Round 4: using C, *1 sc (UKdc) into next sp,
6 dc (UKtr) into next sp*, rep from * to * all
round, join with a sl st to beg of round. Fasten
off and work in all the ends.

HIPPY CHIC BEANIE

Materials:

1 ball each of light worsted (DK/8-ply) merino yarn in lavender, orange, cyclamen, azalea/purple and violet; 50g/142yd/130m

Hook:

Size 3mm (US D, UK 10) crochet hook

Size:

Head circumference 21¼–23in (54–58cm)

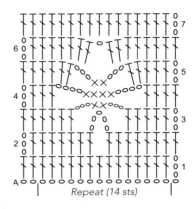

Gauge (tension) sample

18 sts and 11 rows of dc (*UKtr*) using a 3mm (US D, UK 10) crochet hook = 4 x 4in (10 x 10cm). Change your hook if necessary to obtain the correct gauge (tension).

Changing colours

Rows 1–7: lavender; Rows 8–14: orange; Rows 15–21: cyclamen; Rows 22–32: azalea/purple.

Tip

You can crochet this beanie in just one colour using two balls of yarn.

Basic pattern

This hat is worked as a flat piece in rows. Work the 1st dc (*UKtr*) of the row into the 4th ch from the hook. The letter A on the chart marks the start of the foundation ch. The numbers show the start of each row. Start each row with 3 turning ch to replace the 1st dc (*UKtr*). On each row, start by working 1 st before the repeat, work the repeats as required, and finish with 1 st after the final repeat. Rep rows 1–7 to obtain the correct length, making sure the rows align.

Instructions:

Crochet the hat as a flat piece and sew together afterwards at the centre back.

Working in lavender yarn, begin with 90 ch, which includes 3 ch to replace the 1st dc (*UKtr*). Work following the chart and the instructions for the basic pattern, making the colour changes given above. From row 28, work decreases in azalea/purple to make the shape of the hat as follows:

Row 28: 3 ch (= 1st dc/*UKtr*), dc2tog (*UKtr2tog*), * 1 dc (*UKtr*), dc2tog (*UKtr2tog*)* , rep from * to * to end of row (58 sts).

Row 29: 3 ch (= 1st dc/*UKtr*), work 1 dc (*UKtr*) into each st (58 sts).

Row 30: 3 ch (= 1st dc/*UKtr*), work 1 dc (*UKtr*) into every 2nd dc (*UKtr*) of the previous row, skipping the sts in between (29 sts).

Row 31: 3 ch, work 1 dc (*UKtr*) into each st (29 sts).

Row 32: Repeat row 30 (15 sts). Fasten off.

Making up

Draw together the remaining 15 sts with the yarn end, catching in the decrease loop of the dc (*UKtr*) each time. Join the sides to make a centre-back seam and finish off the yarn ends.

Edging

Round 1: Using violet yarn, work *1 sc (*UKdc*) around the next dc (*UKtr*) of the 1st row, pull up the st close to the edge then ch 1, skip 1 dc (*UKtr*)* , repeat from * to * to the end and join the round with a sl st.

Round 2: Work 1 ch then sc (*UKdc*) into each st of the previous round; join into a round with a sl st.

BABY PENGUIN

Materials:

1 ball each of No. 3 crochet cotton in white and black;
   100g/306yd/280m

Small amounts of yellow, blue and silver metallic yarn

Sewing threads to match yarn

Small amount of toy stuffing

Tools:

Size 2mm (US B/1, UK 14) crochet hook

Sewing needle

Size:

Approx. 3in (8.5cm) tall, including hat

Instructions:

Using white crochet cotton, make 2 ch, work 6 sc (*UKdc*) into 2nd ch from hook then join with sl st into a ring.

Round 1: work 2 sc (*UKdc*) into each sc (*UKdc*) to end then join with a sl st.

Round 2: *1 sc (*UKdc*) into next sc (*UKdc*), 2 sc (*UKdc*) into next sc (*UKdc*),* repeat from * to * all around then join with a sl st as before.

Round 3: *1 sc (*UKdc*) into each of next 2 sc (*UKdc*), 2 sc (*UKdc*) into next sc (*UKdc*),* repeat from * to * all around then join with a sl st as before.

Round 4: *1 sc (*UKdc*) into each of next 3 sc (*UKdc*), 2 sc (*UKdc*) into next sc (*UKdc*),* repeat from * to * all around then join with a sl st as before.

Round 5: 1 sc (*UKdc*) into each of next 4 sc (*UKdc*), 2 sc (*UKdc*) into next sc (*UKdc*),* repeat from * to * all around then join with a sl st as before.

Work 4 rounds in sc (*UKdc*) with no increase.

Change to black and work 4 rounds of sc (*UKdc*).

Now shape the top, stuffing the penguin as you go.

Next round: *1 sc (*UKdc*) into each of next 4 sc (*UKdc*), sc (*UKdc*) 2 tog,* repeat from * to * all around then join with a sl st as before.

Next round: *1 sc (*UKdc*) into each of next 3 sc (*UKdc*), sc (*UKdc*) 2 tog,* repeat from * to * all around then join with a sl st as before.

Next round: *1 sc (*UKdc*) into each of next 2 sc (*UKdc*), sc (*UKdc*) 2 tog,* repeat from * to * all around then join with a sl st as before.

Next round: *1 sc (*UKdc*) into next sc (*UKdc*), sc (*UKdc*) 2 tog,* repeat from * to * all around then join with a sl st as before.

Next round: sc (*UKdc*) 2 tog all around. Fasten off and run thread through the last row of sts; draw up and fasten off.

Feet (make 2)

Using yellow, make 7 ch.

Row 1: 1 sc (*UKdc*) into 2nd ch from hook, 1 sc (*UKdc*) into each ch to end, turn (6 sts).

Row 2: 1 ch, work 1 sc (*UKdc*) into each sc (*UKdc*) to end, turn.

Rows 3–4: work in sc (*UKdc*), decreasing 1 sc (*UKdc*) at each end of row.

Rows 5–6: work in sc (*UKdc*) on these 2 sts.

Rows 7–8: work in sc (*UKdc*), increasing 1 sc (*UKdc*) at each end of row.

Work 2 rows in sc (*UKdc*) on these 6 sts then fasten off.

Beak

Using yellow, make 7 ch.

Row 1: 1 sc (*UKdc*) into 2nd ch from hook, 1 sc (*UKdc*) into each ch to end, turn (6 sts).

Rows 2–3: work in sc (*UKdc*), decreasing 1 sc (*UKdc*) at each end of row.

Rows 4–5: work in sc (*UKdc*) on these 2 sts.

Rows 6–7: work in sc (*UKdc*), increasing 1 sc (*UKdc*) at each end of row.

Work 1 row in sc (*UKdc*) on these 6 sts then fasten off.

Wings (make 2)

Using black, make 2 ch.

Row 1: 2 sc (*UKdc*) into 2nd ch from hook, turn.

Row 2: 2 sc (*UKdc*) into first sc (*UKdc*), 1 sc (*UKdc*) into next sc (*UKdc*), turn.

Row 3: 2 sc (*UKdc*) into first sc (*UKdc*), 1 sc (*UKdc*) into next sc (*UKdc*), 2 sc (*UKdc*) into last sc (*UKdc*).

Rows 4–7: work sc (*UKdc*) on these 5 sts.

Rows 8–9: work in sc (*UKdc*), decreasing 1 sc (*UKdc*) at each end of row. Fasten off.

Eyes (make 2)

Using white, make 2 ch, work 6 sc (*UKdc*) into 2nd ch from hook then join with a sl st into a ring.

Round 1: 1 ch, work 2 sc (*UKdc*) into each sc (*UKdc*) all around, join with a sl st.

Round 2: 1 ch, *1 sc (*UKdc*) into next sc (*UKdc*), 2 sc (*UKdc*) into next sc (*UKdc*),* repeat from * to * all around, join with a sl st to beg of round. Fasten off.

Pupils (make 2)

Using black, make 2 ch. Work 6 sc (*UKdc*) into 2nd ch from hook then join with sl st into a circle.

Hat

Using blue, make 21 ch loosely.

Row 1: work 1 dc (*UKtr*) into 3rd ch from hook, 1 dc (*UKtr*) into each ch to end, turn.

Row 2: 3 ch [counts as 1 dc (*UKtr*)], 1 dc (*UKtr*) into each dc (*UKtr*) to end, turn.

Rows 3–5: 3 ch [counts as 1st dc (*UKtr*)], dc (*UKtr*) 2 tog to last st, 1 dc (*UKtr*) in last st. Fasten off.

Join silver metallic yarn to start of hat and work 1 row of sc (*UKdc*) all along the starting ch edge, fasten off.

Hat bobble

Using silver metallic yarn, make 3 ch. Work 12 dc (*UKtr*) into 3rd ch from hook, join with a sl st. Fasten off. Run thread through row of dc (*UKtr*) and draw up tightly into a little ball. Fasten off.

Making up

Work in all ends. Fold each foot in half and sew up the sides – the wide end is the front of the foot. Sew the feet to the base of the body, angling them outwards slightly. Sew a pupil to each eye then work a French knot in white in the centre of each eye. Place the eyes on the body, using the photograph as a guide, and sew in place. Fold the beak in half and sew the sides. Add a little stuffing to pad slightly. Sew the wide end of the beak to the head. Sew a wing to each side of the body. Sew the side seam of the hat and turn back a brim. Sew the bobble to the top. Pop a little stuffing in the hat then stitch it on to the penguin's head.

FREESIA

Materials:

Small amounts of No. 3 crochet cotton in
yellow and green; 100g/306yd/280m

Hook:

Size 3mm (US D, UK 11) crochet hook

Instructions:

Using green crochet cotton, make an adjustable
ring (see page 21).

Round 1: 2 ch, sc (*UKdc*) four times, join with a
sl st into 2 ch.

Round 2: 2 ch, hdc (*UKhtr*) five times into top
stitch of sc (*UKdc*), sl st into 2 ch.

Round 3: repeat round 2. Change to yellow
when sl st into 2 ch.

Round 4: 2 ch, *2 hdc (*UKhtr*) into next ch,1 hdc
(*UKhtr*) into next ch*, repeat from * to * twice
more, 1 hdc (*UKhtr*), sl st into 2 ch.

Petal cluster

In the yellow cotton, *3 ch, tr (*UKdtr*), dtr
(*UKttr*), tr (*UKdtr*), 3 ch, sl st into base hdc
(*UKhtr*), sl st into next hdc (*UKhtr*), sl st into
next hdc (*UKhtr*)*, repeat from * to * three
more times to make 4 petals.

Fasten off and weave in all loose ends.

*Add a touch of springtime to your table
with these pretty little freesias.*

JEFFREY THE DANCING BEAR

Materials:

1 ball of No. 5 crochet cotton in mid-blue, and small amounts in light blue, black and white; 100g/437yd/400m

Black floss for embroidering features

Small amount of metallic yarn in silver

Cocktail stick

Small piece of narrow black satin ribbon for hat band

Toy stuffing

Craft glue

Sewing threads to match crochet cotton

Tools:

Size 2.5mm (US B/1, UK 13) crochet hook

Sewing needle

Instructions:

Make the bear following the instructions on page 37, using mid-blue for the head, body, arms and legs and light blue for the muzzle and ears.

Top hat crown

Round 1: using black yarn, make 2 ch, work 6 sc (UKdc) in 2nd ch, join with a sl st.

Round 2: 2 sc (UKdc) in each sc (UKdc). Join with a sl st to beg of round.

Round 3: *1 sc (UKdc) in next sc (UKdc), 2 sc (UKdc) in next sc (UKdc)*, rep from * to * all round and join as before. Fasten off.

Top hat side

Row 1: using black yarn, make 6 ch, 1 sc (UKdc) in 2nd ch from hook, 1 sc (UKdc) in each ch to end, turn.

Row 2: 1 sc (UKdc) in each sc (UKdc) to end, turn.

Continue on these 5 sts for a further 22 rows. Fasten off.

Brim of hat

Round 1: using black yarn, make 27 ch, join in a circle with a sl st, making sure you do not twist the chain.

Round 2: 1 sc (UKdc) in each ch, join with a sl st to beg of round.

Round 3: 1 sc (UKdc) in first sc (UKdc), *2 sc (UKdc) in next sc (UKdc), 1 sc (UKdc) in next sc (UKdc)*, rep from * to * all round, join as before.

Round 4: sl st in each sc (UKdc) all round. Fasten off.

Bow tie

Using white, make 26 ch, 1 sc (UKdc) in 2nd ch from hook, 1 sc (UKdc) in each ch to end. Fasten off.

Bow

Using white, make 5 ch, 1 sc (UKdc) in 2nd ch from hook, 1 sc (UKdc) in each ch to end.

Next row: 1 ch, 1 sc (UKdc) in each sc (UKdc) to end.

Rep last row twelve times. Fasten off.

Cane

With brown, make 20 ch, turn, 1 sc (UKdc) in 2nd ch from hook, 1 sc (UKdc) in each ch to end. Fasten off.

Making up

Weave in all loose ends. Take the side piece of the top hat and join the two short ends together to form a cylinder. Place the crown on to one end of the cylinder and stitch it carefully in place. Slip the brim over the hat, position it carefully then stitch it in place. Cut a piece of ribbon to fit around the hat, leaving a tiny overlap. Stitch it in place. Stuff the hat lightly and sew it in place. Sew the two short ends of the bow together. Fold it in half with the join at the centre back. Run a thread through from top to bottom at the centre point and draw it up to form a bow shape. Sew the bow to the centre of the bow tie. Secure it around the bear's neck. Place the cocktail stick on to the piece of brown crochet and oversew the two sides together to enclose the wood. Snip off the two sharp points. Wind some metallic thread around one end of the stick to form the silver top. Glue it in place.

LAVENDER HEART

Materials:

1 ball of light worsted (DK/8-ply) cotton in lavender (A) and
    a small amount of green (B); 50g/170yd/155m

Sewing thread

Toy stuffing

Dried lavender

Tools:

Size 3.5mm (US E/4, UK 9) crochet hook

Sewing needle

Notions:

Pearl bead

Size:

From bottom point to centre top between lobes: 2¾in (7cm)

Instructions:

Make 2 hearts

Using yarn A, ch 3 and make 1 turning ch.

Row 1: 1 sc (UKdc) in second ch from hook, 2 sc (UKdc) (3 sts).

Row 2: 1 ch, 2 sc (UKdc) in first st, sc (UKdc) in second st, 2 sc (UKdc) in last st (5 sts).

Row 3: 1 ch, 2 sc (UKdc) in first st, sc (UKdc) to last st, 2 sc (UKdc) in last st (7 sts).

Row 4: 1 ch, 2 sc (UKdc) in first st, sc (UKdc) to last st, 2 sc (UKdc) in last st (9 sts).

Row 5: 1 ch, 2 sc (UKdc) in first st, sc (UKdc) to last st, 2 sc (UKdc) in last st (11 sts).

Row 6: 1 ch, sc (UKdc) across (11 sts).

Rows 7–9: 1 ch, 2 sc (UKdc) in first and last sts and sc (UKdc) in between (17 sts).

Row 10: 1 ch, sc (UKdc) across (17 sts).

Row 11: 1 ch, 2 sc (UKdc) in first st, sc (UKdc) to last st, 2 sc (UKdc) in last st (19 sts).

Row 12: 1 ch, sc (UKdc) across (19 sts).

Row 13: 1 ch, 2 sc (UKdc) in first st, sc (UKdc) to last st, 2 sc (UKdc) in last st (21 sts).

Rows 14 and 15: 1 ch, sc (UKdc) across (21 sts).

Right lobe

Row 16: 1 ch, 10 sc (UKdc), turn.

Row 17: 1 ch, sc (UKdc)2tog, sc (UKdc) to end (9 sts).

Rows 18-20: 1 ch, sc (UKdc)2tog, sc (UKdc) to last 2 sts, sc (UKdc)2tog (3 sts).

Fasten off.

Left lobe

Row 21: Rejoin yarn to the st next to middle st (middle st will remain unworked) and work 10 sc (*UKdc*).

Row 22: 1 ch, sc (*UKdc*) to last 2 sts, sc (*UKdc*)2tog (9 sts).

Rows 23–25: as rows 18–20.

Fasten off.

Making up

With both hearts together, join yarn A to the middle of the heart lobes, work 1 ch and sc (*UKdc*) around the edge, working 2 sts every so often in the same place at the curve of the lobes, and 3 sc (*UKdc*) in the bottom point of the heart to accentuate the shape. Start stuffing the heart when you are halfway round the edge, placing a small amount of dried lavender in the very centre, then continue stuffing as you work. Join the last st to first ch with a sl st and fasten off.

Weave in all loose ends.

Flower

Using yarn A, ch 26, sc (*UKdc*) in second ch from hook and sc (*UKdc*) to end (25 sts).

Row 1: 1 ch, *skip 1 st, 5 hdc (UKhtr) into next st, sl st into next st*, rep to end of row ending with a sl st.

Fasten off with a long tail of yarn, curve the length of crochet round into a flower shape and secure it with a few stitches. Attach it to the centre of the heart with the yarn tail and fasten off. Sew the pearl bead to the centre with the sewing needle and thread.

Leaves (make 2)

With yarn B, ch 8.

Row 1: 1 sc (*UKdc*) in second chain from hook, 1 hdc (*UKhtr*), 1 dc (*UKtr*), 2 dc (*UKtr*) in next ch, 1 dc (*UKtr*), 1 hdc (*UKhtr*), 1 sc (*UKdc*), 2 ch, sl st in second ch from hook to make picot point.

Now work a 'mirror image' of row 1 along the bottom of the foundation chain into the single loops.

Row 2: 1 sc (*UKdc*), 1 hdc (*UKhtr*), 1 dc (*UKtr*), 2 dc (*UKtr*) in next ch, 1 dc (*UKtr*), 1 hdc (*UKhtr*), 1 sc (*UKdc*), sl st into the last ch.

Fasten off, leaving a long tail.

Pin the leaves into position just under the bottom of the flower and, using the long yarn tail, attach them securely to the heart with a few stitches underneath so that they do not show.

Hanging loop

Attach yarn A to the middle of the heart lobes with a sl st, ch 16 and join with a sl st to the middle again. Fasten off and weave in all loose ends.

HIMALAYAN POPPY

Instructions:

Using yarn A, make an adjustable ring, ch 1, work 8 sc (*UKdc*) into ring, and sl st to first st (8 sts).

Round 1: 1 ch, 1 sc (*UKdc*) in same st, 2 sc (*UKdc*) in each around, sl st to ch-1. Fasten off (16 sts).

Round 2: Using yarn B, attach to any st, *4 ch, 1 tr (*UKdtr*) in same st, 2 dtr (*UKtrtr*) in each of next 2 sts, [1 tr (*UKdtr*), 4 ch, sl st] in next st, sl st to next st, rep from * three times. Fasten off.

Round 3: Using yarn C, attach to any petal between the two centre sts, 12 ch, *sl st between centre sts of next petal, 12 ch, rep from * twice more, sl st to first petal.

Round 4: sl st to first 12-ch loop, [3 ch, 2 dc (*UKtr*), 1 ch, 3 dc (*UKtr*), 1 ch, 3 dc (*UKtr*), 1 ch, 3 dc (*UKtr*), 2 ch] in same loop, in remaining three 12-ch loops work [3 dc (*UKtr*), 1 ch] three times, then 3 dc (*UKtr*), 2 ch, sl st to third ch of initial 3-ch.

Round 5: sl st to next 1-ch sp, [3 ch, 2 dc (*UKtr*), 1 ch], [3 dc (*UKtr*), 1 ch], in corner [3 dc (*UKtr*), 2 ch, 3 dc (*UKtr*)]; continue working [3 dc (*UKtr*), 1 ch] in ch-1 spaces along sides of square, and [3 dc (*UKtr*), 2 ch, 3 dc (*UKtr*)] in each corner; at end sl st to third ch of initial 3-ch.

Making up
Fasten off and weave in all loose ends. Block to achieve correct square shape.

Materials:
Small amounts of crochet cotton in yellow (A), turquoise (B), and white (C); 100g/306yd/280m

Hook:
Size 2.5mm (US B/1, UK 13) crochet hook

Size:
Approx. 5½in (14cm) from corner to opposite corner

129

You can try lots of different colour combinations for this poppy, which would be the perfect motif to use for a lovely summer wrap.

LOTTIE PURSE

Instructions:

Make 2 purse motifs

With 3.5mm (US E/4, UK 9) crochet hook make 5 ch, join with sl st to first ch to form a ring.

Round 1: 3 ch (counts as 1 dc (*UKtr*)), 1 dc (*UKtr*) into ring, *1 ch, 2 dc (*UKtr*) into ring, rep from * five more times, 1 ch, sl st in top of 3 ch.

Round 2: sl st to first dc (*UKtr*) and ch sp, 3 ch (counts as 1 dc (*UKtr*)), [1 dc (*UKtr*), 1 ch, 2 dc (*UKtr*)] into same sp, 1 ch, *[2dc (*UKtr*), 1 ch, 2 dc (*UKtr*)] into next ch sp, 1 ch, rep from * four more times, sl st in top of 3 ch.

Round 3: sl st to first dc (*UKtr*) and ch sp, 3 ch (counts as 1 dc (*UKtr*)), 2 dc (*UKtr*) into same ch sp, 1 ch, *3 dc (*UKtr*) into next ch sp, 1 ch, rep from * to end, sl st in top of 3 ch.

Round 4: sl st to next 2 dc (*UKtr*) and ch sp, 3 ch (counts as 1 dc (*UKtr*)), 2 dc (*UKtr*) into same ch sp, 1 ch, *3 dc (*UKtr*) into next ch sp, 1 ch, rep from * to end, sl st in top of 3 ch.

Round 5: sl st to next 2 dc (*UKtr*) and ch sp, 3 ch (counts as 1 dc (*UKtr*)), 1 dc (*UKtr*) into same ch sp, 1 ch, *[2dc (*UKtr*), 1 ch, 2 dc (*UKtr*)] into next ch sp, 1 ch, rep from * five more times, 2 dc (*UKtr*) into next ch sp.

Fasten off yarn.

Shell edge

With RS facing, attach yarn to top of 3 ch at beg of last round, 1 ch, *6 dc (*UKtr*) into next ch sp, 1 sc (*UKdc*) into next ch sp, rep from * five more times, 6 dc (*UKtr*) into next ch sp, 1 sc (*UKdc*) to top of last dc (*UKtr*) from previous round.

Making up

Weave in all loose ends. Attach the narrower parts of the circle to the purse clasp and sew together around the shell edging. Sew the lining to the inside of the purse, leaving a ½in (1cm) seam allowance.

Materials:

1 ball of fingering (4-ply) yarn in red; 50g/197yd/180m

2 x pieces of fabric for lining, approx. 4in (10cm) in diameter (optional)

Hook:

Size 3.5mm (US E/4, UK 9) crochet hook

Notions:

1 x rounded purse clasp approx. 3⅜in (8.5cm) wide

Size:

Approx. 4¾in (12cm) at the widest point and 4in (10cm) in height

CATHERINE WHEEL

Materials:

Small amounts of No. 3 crochet cotton in pale green (A), purple
   (B) and lilac (C); 100g/306yd/280m

Hook:

Size 3mm (US D, UK 10) crochet hook

Size:

4in (10cm) in diameter

Instructions:

Using A, make 6 ch, join into a circle with a sl st.

Round 1: using A, 1 ch, work 12 sc (*UKdc*) into circle, join
with a sl st.

Round 2: using B, 3 ch, 1 dc (*UKtr*) into same sp, leave last
loop on hook, draw through both loops, 2 ch, *2 dc (*UKtr*)
into next dc, leaving last loop on hook, yrh, draw through
both loops, 2 ch*, rep from * to * all round, joining to top of
first dc (*UKtr*) at beg of round. Fasten off yarn B.

Round 3: using C, sl st into first 2 ch, 1 sc (*UKdc*) into sp, 3
ch,1 sc (*UKdc*) into next sp, *3 ch, 1 sc (*UKdc*) into next sp*,
rep from * to * all round, 3 ch, sl st to beg of round.

Round 4: using C, sl st into first 3 ch sp, 3 ch, 2 dc (*UKtr*)
into same sp, leaving last loop on hook, yrh, draw through
all loops on hook, *4 ch, 3 dc (*UKtr*) into next sp, leaving
last loop on hook, yrh, draw through all loops*, rep from *
to * all round, join with a sl st to top of 3 ch at beg of round.
Fasten off yarn C.

Round 5: using A, sl st into next 4 ch sp, 3 ch, 3 dc (*UKtr*)
into same sp, 3 ch, 4 dc (*UKtr*) into same sp, *1 ch, 4 dc
(*UKtr*) into next sp, 1 ch, 4 dc (*UKtr*) into next sp, 1 ch, [4 dc
(*UKtr*), 3 ch, 4 dc (*UKtr*)] into next sp*, rep from * to * twice
more, 1 ch, 4 dc (*UKtr*) into next sp, 1 ch, 4 dc (*UKtr*) into
next sp, 1 ch, join with a sl st to dc (*UKtr*) at beg of round.
Fasten off yarn A.

Round 6: using B, 1 sc (*UKdc*) into each dc (*UKtr*) all round
and 4 sc (*UKdc*) into each corner sp, join with a sl st to beg
of round. Fasten off and weave in all loose ends.

LADY GREY BEANIE

Materials:

2 balls of light worsted (DK/8-ply) merino/
acrylic blend yarn in dusty grey;
50g/126yd/115m

Hooks:

Size 4mm (US G/6, UK 8) and 5mm (US H/8,
UK 6) crochet hooks

Size:

Head circumference
21¼–23in (54–58cm)

Gauge (tension) sample

2 repeats and 15 rows in the basic pattern using the
5mm (US H/8, UK 6) crochet hook = 4 x 4in (10 x 10cm).
Change your hook if necessary to obtain the correct
gauge (tension).

Basic pattern

The hat is worked in rows following the chart. The
pattern can be worked over a multiple of 6 sts + 2
(including 1 turning ch). The numbers on each side show
the start of the row each time. Each row starts with the
number of ch corresponding to the st height, as shown.
Start each row with the st before the repeat, work the
repeats as required and finish with the st after the final
repeat. Work rows 1–6, then keep repeating rows 3–6
until the desired length is obtained. Work the bobbles as
follows in odd-numbered rows.

Bobble: Work 3 dc (UKtr) into the same st, yrh and draw
through all 3 sts together.

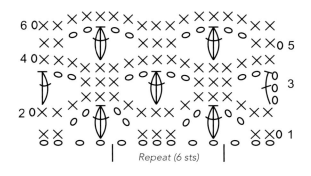

Repeat (6 sts)

Instructions:

Crochet the beanie as a flat piece in rows, working from
the bottom edge up to the crown. Sew together at the
centre back afterwards.

Begin by working 68 ch loosely (includes 1 turning ch)
using the 5mm (US H/8, UK 6) crochet hook.

Rows 1–26: Follow the chart to work in the basic pattern
(11 repeats).

Row 27 (decrease round): 3 ch (= 1st dc/UKtr), 1 dc
(UKtr) into the 1st sc (UKdc) of the previous row, * 1 ch,
1 bobble st into every 4th sc (UKdc) of the previous row
*, rep from * to * to end of row, finishing with 1 ch and
2 dc (UKtr) into the last sc (UKdc).

Row 28: 1 ch, then work 1 sc (UKdc) into each st and
around every ch of the previous row.

Row 29: 3 ch (= 1st dc/UKtr), then work 1 dc (UKtr) into
each 2nd dc (UKtr) of the previous row (30 sts).

Row 30: 3 ch (=1st dc/UKtr), then work dc2tog
(UKtr2tog) to end of row. Draw the remaining 15 sts
together with the yarn end, catching in the decrease
loops each time.

Join the edges of the piece together to create the
centre-back seam.

Change to the 4mm (US G/6, UK8) hook and work the
bottom band in rounds of hdc (UKhtr) as follows:

Round 1: 2 ch (counts as 1st hdc/UKhtr), work 1 hdc
(UKhtr) into every ch of the foundation ch, close up with
a sl st into the 1st st of the round (67 sts).

Rows 2–4: 2 ch (counts as 1st hdc/UKhtr), work hdc
(UKhtr) into every st around, close up with a sl st into the
1st st of the round. Fasten off and weave in loose ends.

COOL SNOWMAN

Materials:

1 ball of No. 3 crochet cotton in white, and
    small amounts of black, green and orange;
    100g/306yd/280m

Scrap of mini tinsel

4 x tiny black buttons

Sewing thread to match the yarn

Small amount of toy stuffing

Tools:

Size 2mm (US B/1, UK 14) crochet hook

Sewing needle

Size:

Approx. 4in (10cm) tall

Instructions:

Head

Using white crochet cotton, make 2 ch.

Round 1: work 6 sc (*UKdc*) into 2nd ch from hook then join with a sl st to form a tight circle.

Round 2: work 2 sc (*UKdc*) into each st around then join with a sl st.

Round 3: *1 sc (*UKdc*) into next sc (*UKdc*), 2 sc (*UKdc*) into next sc (*UKdc*),* repeat from * to * all around then join with a sl st as before.

Round 4: *1 sc (*UKdc*) into each of next 2 sc (*UKdc*), 2 sc (*UKdc*) into next sc (*UKdc*),* repeat from * to * all around then join with a sl st.

Rounds 5–9: work in sc (*UKdc*) all around.

You will now begin decreasing. Stuff the head before you close it up.

Round 10: *1 sc (*UKdc*) into each of next 2 sc (*UKdc*), sc (*UKdc*) 2 tog,* repeat from * to * all around then join with a sl st as before.

Round 11: work in sc (*UKdc*) all around.

Round 12: *1 sc (*UKdc*) into next sc (*UKdc*), sc (*UKdc*) 2 tog,* repeat from * to * all around then join with a sl st.

Round 13: work in sc (*UKdc*) all around.

Round 14: sc (*UKdc*) 2 tog all around then join with a sl st. Fasten off.

Body

Using white crochet cotton, make 2 ch.

Round 1: work 6 sc (*UKdc*) into 2nd ch from hook then join with a sl st to form a tight circle.

Round 2: 2 sc (*UKdc*) into each st around then join with a sl st (12 sts).

Round 3: *1 sc (*UKdc*) into next sc (*UKdc*), 2 sc (*UKdc*) into next sc (*UKdc*),* repeat from * to * all around then join with a sl st.

Round 4: *1 sc (*UKdc*) into each of next 2 sc (*UKdc*), 2 sc (*UKdc*) into next sc (*UKdc*),* repeat from * to * all around then join with a sl st.

Round 5: *1 sc (*UKdc*) into each of next 3 sc (UKdc), 2 sc (*UKdc*) into next sc (*UKdc*),* repeat from * to * all around then join with a sl st.

Rounds 6–20 work in sc (*UKdc*) all around.
Fasten off.

Base

Using white crochet cotton, make 2 ch.

Round 1: work 6 sc (*UKdc*) into 2nd ch from hook then join with a sl st to form a tight circle.

Round 2: 2 sc (*UKdc*) into each st around then join with a sl st.

Round 3: *1 sc (*UKdc*) into next sc (*UKdc*), 2 sc (*UKdc*) into next sc (*UKdc*),* repeat from * to * all around then join with a sl st.

Round 4: *1 sc (*UKdc*) into each of next 2 sc (UKdc), 2 sc (*UKdc*) into next sc (*UKdc*),* repeat from * to * all around then join with a sl st.

Work 1 round in sc (*UKdc*). Fasten off.

Hat

Using black crochet cotton, make 2 ch.

Round 1: work 6 sc (*UKdc*) into 2nd ch from hook then join with a sl st to form a tight circle.

Round 2: 2 sc (*UKdc*) into each st around then join with a sl st (12 sts).

Round 3: *1 sc (*UKdc*) into next sc (*UKdc*), 2 sc (*UKdc*) into next sc (*UKdc*),* repeat from * to * all around then join with a sl st (18 sts).

Rounds 4–5: work in sc (*UKdc*) all around.

Round 6: work 2 sc (*UKdc*) into each sc (*UKdc*) all around then join with a sl st.

Round 7: work in sc (*UKdc*) all around. Fasten off.

Scarf

Using green crochet cotton, make 36 ch.

Row 1: work 1 sc (*UKdc*) into 2nd ch from hook, 1 sc (*UKdc*) into each ch to end.

Rows 2–3: work in sc (*UKdc*) to end. Fasten off.

Making up

Work in all the ends. Stuff the body lightly and then sew the base to the body. Invert the base slightly to make the snowman stand up. Sew the hat on to the head. Embroider the features with black and orange, using the photograph as a guide. Now attach the head to the body. Sew the buttons to the front of the snowman. Wrap mini tinsel around the hat and secure with a stitch. Wrap the scarf around the snowman's neck and secure with a few stitches. Make a hanging loop by crocheting a chain of black cotton, if required, and attach it to the top of the hat.

DAISY CHAIN

Materials:

No. 3 crochet cotton in yellow and white
27½in (70cm) silver-plated cable jewellery chain
39½in (100cm) green sheer organza ribbon
Sewing thread

Tools:

Size 2.5mm (US B/1, UK 13) crochet hook
Sewing needle

Instructions:

Single daisy

With yellow crochet cotton, make an adjustable ring (see page 21).

Round 1: 1 ch, 8 sc (*UKdc*) into ring, pull end to close ring and remove hook.

Re-insert hook from back of work into first sc (*UKdc*) loop with a sl st.

Round 2: change to white crochet cotton, *3 ch, sl st into back of each of these 3 ch, sl st into next base sc (*UKdc*)*, repeat from * to * seven times, making eight petals altogether.

Sl st to centre and tie off the ends.

Double daisy

Follow the instructions for the single daisy up to the end of round 2.

Round 3: work into base sl st between petals 1 and 2 of round 2, *sc (*UKdc*), 3 ch, sl st into back of each of 3 ch to base ch*, repeat from * to * seven more times.

sc (*UKdc*) to centre and tie off the ends.

Make seven daisies (some single and some double). Thread the green ribbon through the looped silver necklace and tie it in a knot at the back. Stitch daisies on to the ribbon at regular intervals.

Who could resist this pretty necklace made with hand-crocheted daisies? Alternatively, make them into a stunning hairband or bracelet.

SPARKLES THE FAIRY BEAR

Materials:

- 1 ball of No. 5 crochet cotton in mid-pink, and a small amount in dark pink; 100g/437yd/400m
- Small amount of gold metallic yarn
- Dark brown floss for embroidering features
- Toy stuffing
- 7 small sequin stars
- Piece of pink net for skirt, 7 x 4¾in (18 x 12cm)
- Cocktail stick
- 3 adhesive gold, sparkly stars
- Sewing threads to match crochet cotton
- Craft glue

Tools:

- Size 2.5mm (US B/1, UK 13) crochet hook
- Sewing needle

Instructions:

Make the bear following the basic instructions on page 37, using mid-pink for the head, body, arms and legs and dark pink for the muzzle and ears.

Wings (make 2)

Row 1: using gold metallic yarn, make 3 ch, 9 dc (*UKtr*) in 3rd ch from hook, turn.

Row 2: 3 ch, 1 dc (*UKtr*) in first dc (*UKtr*), 2 dc (*UKtr*) in each rem dc (*UKtr*), turn.

Row 3: 1 sc (*UKdc*) in each dc (*UKtr*) to end. Fasten off.

Skirt

Take the piece of net and fold it in half lengthwise, the folded edge forming the bottom of the skirt. Using a sewing needle and matching thread, lightly gather the net to fit around the bear's waist. Secure the thread firmly to ensure the skirt remains gathered.

Using pink crochet cotton, work a row of sc (*UKdc*) along the top edge of the skirt, working through both thicknesses of net.

Turn, and work a further row of sc (*UKdc*). Fasten off.

Headdress

Using metallic yarn, make 4 ch, join in a circle with a sl st.

Next row: *4 ch, 1 sc (*UKdc*) in circle*, rep from * to * five times, join with a sl st to beg of row. Fasten off.

Making up

Make the wand by wrapping the cocktail stick tightly with a length of metallic yarn, leaving a small section at one end uncovered to enable you to stick on the star. Secure the ends of the yarn with craft glue. Take two adhesive stars and press them together firmly, one on each side of the top of the stick. Secure the wand in the bear's paw by threading it through the crochet stitches. Sew the wings together firmly at the centre. Place them in the middle of the bear's back and secure. Sew small sequin stars randomly over the net skirt. Place the skirt around the bear's waist and sew the crochet band together at the centre back. Finally, work in the ends of the crocheted headdress and attach an adhesive star firmly to the centre. Sew the headdress to the top of the bear's head with some tiny stitches.

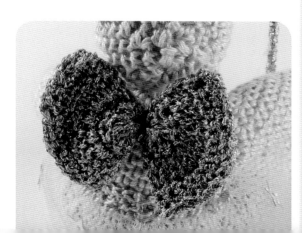

HEART BOOKMARK

Materials:
Small amount of No. 5
   crochet cotton in kingfisher;
   100g/437yd/400m

Tools:
Size 2.5mm (US B/1, UK 13)
   crochet hook

Notions:
5 small turquoise beads

Size:
13¾in (35cm) from point
   between heart lobes to end
   of tassel

Instructions:

Ch 5 and join with a sl st to make a ring.

Round 1: Ch 3 (counts as first dc (*UKtr*)), 2 dc (*UKtr*) into ring, 2 ch, [3 dc (*UKtr*), 2 ch] into ring three more times. Join with a sl st to top of beginning 3-ch (12 dc (*UKtr*), four 2-ch sps).

Round 2: Sl st in next 2 sts and into 2-ch sp, 3 ch (counts as first dc (*UKtr*)), [2 dc (*UKtr*), 2 ch, 3 dc (*UKtr*)] in 2-ch sp, 2 ch, *skip next 3 dc (*UKtr*) and work 3 dc (*UKtr*), 2 ch, 3 dc (*UKtr*) in next 2-ch sp, 2 ch;* rep from * to * twice more; join with a sl st to initial 3-ch.

Round 3: Sl st in next 2 sts and into 2-ch sp; *1 ch, 1 dc (*UKtr*) into next 2-ch sp (centre of the square), 1 ch, [1 dc (*UKtr*), 1 ch] six more times in same 2-ch space, join with a sl st in next 2-ch sp*. One lobe of the heart is now completed. Rep from * to * to make second lobe.

Fasten off.

Round 4: Rejoin yarn at the bottom of the heart, just to the right of the point, make 1 ch, and sc (*UKdc*) round into sts and ch-sps, working 2 sc (*UKdc*) into the 2-ch sp. At the dip between the two heart lobes, make a sl st in the middle, then continue in sc (*UKdc*). At the bottom point of the heart, work 1 sc (*UKdc*), 1 dc (*UKtr*), 1 sc (*UKdc*) into the point and finish with a sl st into the first ch at beg of round.

Fasten off and weave in all loose ends.

Tail

Rejoin yarn at the bottom point of the heart and make 35 ch, sc (*UKdc*) into second st from hook and sc (*UKdc*) to end, sl st back to point and fasten off.

Tassel

Wind a length of yarn round your four fingers held together nine or ten times and cut the end. Now cut through the loops at one end and thread through a tapestry needle. Push the needle through the bottom of the tail and pull so that the yarn is even on both sides. Tie another length of yarn round the top, just below the end of the tail, to secure the top of the tassel. Now thread some small blue beads onto several threads so that they hang at different heights and tie a knot below the beads to secure them. Block the heart and tail if desired.

The motifs for this pillow were worked in black (A), seville (B), sunflower (C) and azure (D) using Stylecraft Classique cotton DK yarn; 100g/201yd/184m. Make six motifs, using yarn C for rounds 2, 3 and 4. Block if desired. Join the edges of the motifs together with yarn D, using single crochet (UKdc). Pin the resulting rectangle to a pillow pad of the same size, and sew it to the pad with turquoise thread, making small, neat stitches just under the edge of the crochet, so that they do not show.

SUNFLOWER

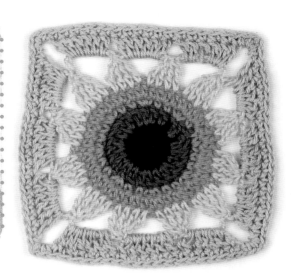

Materials:
Small amounts of No. 3 crochet cotton in black (A), brown (B), orange (C), yellow (D) and mid-green (E); 100g/306yd/280m

Tools:
Size 2.5mm (US B/1, UK 13) crochet hook

Size:
One motif is approx. 6in (15cm) from corner to opposite corner

Special stitch

The 4-tr (*UKdtr*) cluster stitch is worked as follows: 5 ch (counts as 1 tr (*UKdtr*)) – yrh twice, insert hook into next st, yrh and pull through 2 loops, yrh and pull through 2 loops (2 loops left on hook), yrh twice, insert hook into next st, yrh and pull through 2 loops, yrh and pull through 2 loops, (3 loops left on hook), yrh twice, insert hook into next st, yrh and pull through 2 loops, yrh and pull through 2 loops (4 loops left on hook), yrh and pull through all 4 loops, make a sl st to complete the cluster.

Instructions:

Using yarn A, ch 4, 15 dc (*UKtr*) in fourth ch from hook, sl st to third ch of initial 4-ch. Fasten off (16 sts).

Round 1: Using yarn B, join to any st. 3 ch, 2 dc (*UKtr*) in next st, *1 dc (*UKtr*), in next st, 2 dc (*UKtr*) in next st, rep from * to end. Fasten off (24 sts).

Round 2: Using yarn C, join to any st, 1 ch, *1 sc (*UKdc*) in each of next 2 sts, 2 sc (*UKdc*) in next st, rep from * to end, sl st to initial ch (32 sts).

Round 3: 2 ch, 2 hdc (*UKhtr*) in next st, *1 hdc (*UKhtr*) in next st, 2 hdc (*UKhtr*) in next st, rep from * to end, sl st to initial 2-ch. Fasten off (48 sts).

Round 4: Using yarn D, join to any st, *[5 ch, work a 3-tr (*UKdtr*) cluster in next 3 sts], 5 ch, work a 4-tr (*UKdtr*) cluster to end, sl st to fifth st of initial 5-ch. Fasten off (12 petals).

Round 5: Using yarn E, attach yarn to any 5-ch sp, 6 ch, work [6 dc (*UKtr*) in next two 5-ch sps, 3 ch], work *[6 dc (*UKtr*) in next three 5-ch sps, 3 ch] three times; in last sp, 5 dc (*UKtr*) and sl st to third ch of initial 6-ch.

Round 6: 1 ch, work 3 sc (*UKdc*) in each 3-ch sp and 1 sc (*UKdc*) in each st around, sl st to initial 1-ch.

Making up

Fasten off and weave in all loose ends. Block to achieve an even square shape.

BOBBLES PURSE

Materials:
1 ball of worsted yarn (UK light aran) in gold; 100g/219yd/200m

Hook:
4mm (US G/6, UK 8) crochet hook

Notions:
1 x rounded purse clasp approx. 3¼in (8½cm) wide

Size:
Approx. 5in (13cm) wide and 6in (15cm) high

Special abbreviations:
Tr5tog (*UKdtr5tog*) cluster: [yrh twice and insert into st, yrh and draw a loop through, yrh and draw through first 2 loops on hook, yrh and draw through next 2 loops on hook] rep four times all in the same st, yrh and draw a loop through all 6 loops on hook.

Tr6tog (*UKdtr6tog*) cluster: [yrh twice and insert into st, yrh and draw a loop through, yrh and draw through first 2 loops on hook, yrh and draw through next 2 loops on hook] rep five times all in the same st, yrh and draw a loop through all 7 loops on hook.

Instructions:

Make 2 purse motifs
With 4mm (US G/6, UK 8) crochet hook make 20 ch.

Row 1: Tr5tog (*UKdtr5tog*) in fourth ch from hook, *2 ch, skip 1 ch, 1 sc (*UKdc*) in next ch, *2 ch, skip 1 ch, tr6tog (*UKdtr6tog*) in next ch, rep from * to end.

Row 2: 2 ch, 1 sc (*UKdc*) in base of ch, 2 ch, tr5tog (*UKdtr5tog*) in next sc (*UKdc*), 2 ch, 1 sc (*UKdc*) in top of next cluster, *2 ch, tr6tog (*UKdtr6tog*) in next sc (*UKdc*), 2 ch, 1 sc (UKdc) in top of next cluster, rep from * to end.

Row 3: 3 ch, tr6tog (*UKdtr6tog*) in base of 3-ch, *2 ch, 1 sc (*UKdc*) in top of next cluster, 2 ch, tr6tog (*UKdtr6tog*) in next sc (*UKdc*), rep from * to end.

Repeat rows 2 and 3 twice more, then row 2 once.

Start of top shaping
Row 1: 1 ch, *2 sc (*UKdc*) in 2-ch sp, 1 sc (*UKdc*) in top of next cluster, skip 2 ch and 1 sc (*UKdc*), rep from * to end (12 sts).

Row 2: 1 ch, 1 sc (*UKdc*) in each st to end.

Rep row 2 twice more.

Row 5: 1 ch, sc2tog (*UKdc2tog*), 1 sc (*UKdc*) in each st to last 2 sts, sc2tog (*UKdc2tog*) (10 sts).

Rep row 2 once more.

Rep row 5 (8 sts).

Rep row 2.

Fasten off yarn.

Making up
Using mattress stitch and with WS together, sew the front and back pieces together along the two sides and the bottom of the purse. Turn it through, then attach the clasp to the top. Attach a lining to the inside of the purse if desired.

CIRCLE IN A SQUARE

Materials:
Small amounts of No. 3
    crochet cotton in orange (A),
    white (B) and yellow (C);
    100g/306yd/280m

Hook:
Size 3mm (US D, UK 10)
    crochet hook

Size:
2½in (6.5cm) across

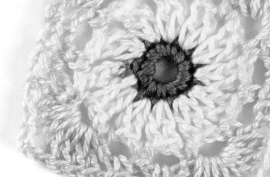

Instructions:

Using A, make 6 ch, join into a circle with a sl st.

Round 1: work 12 sc (*UKdc*) into circle, join with a sl st to beg of round. Fasten off yarn A.

Round 2: using B, 3 ch, 1dc (*UKtr*) into the same sp, *2 ch, 2 dc (*UKtr*) into next sc (*UKdc*)*, rep from * to * all round, ending 2 ch, sl st to top of 3 ch at beg of round. Fasten off yarn B.

Round 3: using C, 1 sc (*UKdc*) into next 2 ch sp, *4 ch, 1 sc (*UKdc*) into next 2 ch sp*, rep from * to * all round, ending last rep with 4 ch, sl st to beg of round.

Round 4: sl st into next 4 ch sp, 3 ch, 3 dc (*UKtr*), 3 ch, 4 dc (*UKtr*) into same sp, *2 ch, 1 sc (*UKdc*) into next sp, 2 ch, 1 sc (*UKdc*) into next sp, 2 ch, 4 dc (*UKtr*), 2 ch, 4 dc (*UKtr*) into next sp*, rep from * to * twice more, ending last rep with 2 ch, 1 sc (*UKdc*) into next sp, 2 ch, 1 sc (*UKdc*) into next sp, 2 ch, sl st into dc (*UKtr*) at beg of round. Fasten off and weave in all loose ends.

COLOUR CLASH BEANIE

Materials:

1 ball each of bulky (chunky) acrylic/
wool blend easy-care yarn in burgundy,
lavender, neon orange, fire red and
purple; 50g/60yd/55m

Hook:

Size 7mm (US K/10½, UK 2)

Size:

Head circumference 21¼–23in
(54–58cm)

Gauge (tension) sample

7 sts and 5 rounds of dc (*UKtr*) using a 7mm (US L/11,
UK 2) crochet hook = 4 x 4in (10 x 10cm). Change your
hook if necessary to obtain the correct gauge (tension).

Basic pattern

Work in rounds of dc (*UKtr*). Start every round with 3 ch,
which represents the 1st dc (*UKtr*), and end every round
with a sl st into the 3rd ch from the start of the round.

Changing colours

Work 1 round each in burgundy, lavender, neon orange,
fire red and purple. Repeat the colours in order until the
beanie is the desired size.

NB: For the colour change, the new colour should be
introduced on the last loop of the previous st to give a
perfect colour transition. In this case, the final st of each
round is a sl st, which should therefore be worked in the
next colour.

Tip

To save on buying lots of different balls of wool – or if
you simply like a plainer style – the hat can be made in
just one colour using two balls of yarn, or in two or three
colours, using one ball of each.

Instructions:

Start the beanie at the crown and work down to the
bottom edge in rounds.

Begin with 3 ch in burgundy then join into a ring with a
sl st. Now work as follows:

Round 1 (burgundy): 3 ch, work 11 dc (*UKtr*) into the
ring. Close up this and all subsequent rounds with a sl
st in the next colour.

Round 2 (lavender): Work 2 dc (*UKtr*) into each st
around (24 sts).

Round 3 (neon orange): 3 ch, 2 dc (*UKtr*) into the next
st, * 1 dc (*UKtr*) into the next st then 2 dc (*UKtr*) into the
next st * , rep from * to * around (36 sts).

Round 4 (fire red): 3 ch, 1 dc (*UKtr*) into each st around
(36 sts).

Rounds 5–14: Following the same colour order, work
1 dc (*UKtr*) into each st around, replacing the 1st dc
(*UKtr*) with 3 ch each time.

Round 15 (purple): 1 ch, sc (*UKdc*) into each st around
then join up the round with a sl st.

Round 16 (burgundy): Work rev sc (*UKrev dc*) into each
st around then fasten off the yarn and darn in the ends.
To work rev sc (*UKrev dc*), simply work from left to right
instead of from right to left (see page 23).

CHRISTMAS CRACKER

Materials:

- 1 ball each of No. 5 crochet cotton in green and red; 100g/437yd/400m
- 40in (1m) of narrow red satin ribbon
- 20in (0.5m) of gold ric-rac braid
- 1 gold rose embellishment
- Small piece of card

Small amount of stuffing

Sewing thread to match the yarn

Tools:

Size 2mm (US B/1, UK 14) crochet hook

Sewing needle

Size:

Approx. 5½in (14cm) long.

Instructions:

Using green crochet cotton, make 27 ch.

Row 1: work 1 dc (*UKtr*) into 3rd ch from hook, 1 dc (*UKtr*) into each ch to end, turn.

Row 2: 1 ch, work 1 sc (*UKdc*) into each dc (*UKtr*) to end, turn.

Row 3: 3 ch, skip first st, work 1 dc (*UKtr*) into each sc (*UKdc*) to end, turn.

Row 4: repeat row 2.

Change to red cotton.

Rows 5–14: repeat rows 3 and 4 five times.

Change to green cotton.

Rows 15–18: repeat rows 3 and 4 twice. Fasten off.

Making up

Work in the ends. Fold the crochet lengthways to form a tube and then sew the long edges together, matching the colours and rows. The seam will be on the underside of the piece.

Measure a piece of card slightly shorter than the inner red section of the cracker. Roll it into a tube then try the tube inside the crochet to get a good fit. When you are happy with the size, glue the edges of the card together and slip the tube inside the cracker.

Add some stuffing to the inside of the tube to give the cracker more body. Cut the red ribbon into two lengths and tie one tightly to each end of the cracker either side of the tube section, using the photograph as a guide. Trim the ribbon if necessary for a smart finish. Measure a piece of gold ric-rac braid long enough to fit around the central red section and glue it in place with the join on the underside. Glue the gold rose embellishment to the centre as shown in the photograph.

Tip

Hide the join on the ric-rac braid under the rose embellishment for a super-neat finish.

AFRICAN VIOLETS

Materials:

Small amounts of No. 3 crochet cotton in violet, yellow and green; 100g/306yd/280m

Sewing thread

Tools:

Size 2.5mm (US B/1, UK 13) crochet hook

Sewing needle

Instructions:

With violet crochet cotton, make 4 ch, ss into a circle.

*1 ch, dc (*UKtr*), tr (*UKdtr*), dc (*UKtr*), 1 ch, ss, all into loop*, repeat from * to * four more times to make 5 petals.

Fasten off the end and press the flower.

Change to yellow crochet cotton and make the central stamen.

3 ch, skip 2 ch, sc (*UKdc*) into ch, ss into base chain.

Fasten off.

Insert the yellow stamen into the centre of the flower and sew it in place with sewing thread.

Leaf

With green crochet cotton, make an adjustable ring (see page 21), 2 ch, 6 sc (*UKdc*), pull to join, ss into 2 ch.

Round 1: 2 ch, then 2 dc (*UKtr*) into each sc (*UKdc*) six times, turn.

Round 2: 2 sc (*UKdc*) into each dc (*UKtr*) twelve times, 1 sc (*UKdc*) into 2 ch, 2 dc (*UKtr*) into 2 ch, 1 sc (*UKdc*) into 2 ch, ss into 2 ch.

Fasten off and weave in all loose ends.

Bring a forgotten yet much-loved possession back to life with these brightly coloured flowers.

MAZZY THE KEEP-FIT BEAR

Materials:

1 ball of No. 5 crochet cotton in beige and
small amounts in ecru, black, lilac and
dark pink; 100g/437yd/400m

Toy stuffing

Black floss for embroidering features

Sewing threads to match crochet cotton

Tools:

Size 2.5mm (US B/1, UK 13)
crochet hook

Sewing needle

Instructions:

Make the bear following the instructions on page 37,
using beige for the head and legs, lilac for the body and
ecru for the muzzle and ears. For each arm, work the
first 10 rows in beige, then change to lilac and complete
the rest of the arm.

Leg warmers (make 2)

Row 1: using dark pink, make 18 ch, 1 dc (*UKtr*) in 3rd ch
from hook, 1 dc (*UKtr*) in each ch to end, turn.

Row 2: 3 ch, skip 1 dc (*UKtr*), 1 dc (*UKtr*) in each dc
(*UKtr*) to end.

Row 3: rep row 2.

Row 4: 1 ch, 1 sc (*UKdc*) in each dc (*UKtr*) to end.
Fasten off.

Headband

Using dark pink, make 30 ch, break pink and join in lilac,
work 1 sc (*UKdc*) in 2nd ch from hook, 1 sc (*UKdc*) in
each ch to end, break lilac and turn.

Join in dark pink, sl st in each sc (*UKdc*) to end.
Fasten off.

Sports bag, front and back

Row 1: using dark pink, make 13 ch, 1 sc (*UKdc*) in 2nd
ch from hook, 1 sc (*UKdc*) in each ch to end, turn.

Row 2: 1 ch, 1 sc (*UKdc*) in each sc (*UKdc*) to end, turn.

Repeat row 2 eighteen times. Fasten off.

Bag handles (make 2)

Using black, make 18 ch. Fasten off.

Bag strap

Using black, make 38 ch. Fasten off.

Arm bands (make 2)

Using dark pink, make 18 ch. Fasten off.

Neck band

Using dark pink, make 30 ch. Fasten off.

Making up

Sew the arm bands on to the arms, where the colour
changes from beige to lilac. Arrange the neck band
around the bear's neck so that it is scooped slightly
at the front, and attach it to the body with one or two
small stitches. Join the headband in a circle and place it
on the bear's head. Secure with a few tiny stitches. Take
the main piece of the sports bag, fold it in half and sew
the side seams. Stuff it lightly with a little stuffing to
give it shape and close the top. Sew a handle to either
side of the bag and attach the strap at either end. Fold
the leg warmers in half lengthways and sew the side
seam. Slip them on to the bear's legs.

CHUNKY HEART PILLOW

Instructions:

This heart is worked from the bottom point upwards.

Ch 2 and work 4 sc (*UKdc*) in second ch from hook.

Now work in a spiral, making *1 sc (*UKdc*), 2 sc (*UKdc*) in next st*, and rep until you have 24 sts; place stitch marker in the last st.

Next round: work 1 sc (*UKdc*) in each st around. Replace marker in the last st.

Next round: *1 sc (*UKdc*) in next 2 sts, 2 sc (*UKdc*) in next st*, rep until you have 32 sts. Place marker.

Next 3 rounds: work 1 sc (*UKdc*) in each st around, moving marker up as you make each round.

Next round: *1 sc (*UKdc*) in next 2 sts, 2 sc (*UKdc*) in next st* until you have 40 sts. Move marker.

Next 3 rounds: work 1 sc (*UKdc*) in each st around, moving marker up as you make each round.

First lobe

Keep using the stitch marker to mark the beginning of a new round.

Next round: sc (*UKdc*) in next 10 sts, skip 20 sts, sc (*UKdc*) in last 10 sts (20 sts).

Next round: work 1 sc (*UKdc*) in each st around (20 sts).

**Next round: sc (*UKdc*) in next 7 sts, [sc (*UKdc*)2tog x 3], sc (*UKdc*) in next 7 sts (17 sts).

Next round: sc (*UKdc*) in next 5 sts, [sc (*UKdc*)2tog x 3], sc (UKdc) in next 6 sts (14 sts).

Materials:

2 balls of super bulky (super chunky) acrylic yarn in bluebell; 100g/52yd/48m

Toy stuffing

Tools:

Size 12mm (US P) crochet hook

Stitch marker

Large-eyed tapestry needle

Size:

From bottom point to centre top between lobes: 8⅝in (22cm)

Next round: sc (*UKdc*) in next 4 sts, [sc (*UKdc*)2tog x 3], sc (*UKdc*) in next 4 sts (11 sts).

Next round: sc (*UKdc*) in next 2 sts, [sc (*UKdc*)2tog x 3], sc (*UKdc*) in next 3 sts (8 sts).

Cut a long tail and thread onto a large-eyed tapestry needle. Catch the front loop of each rem st, going from inside outwards. Then pull the yarn taut to close the hole at the top of the lobe and push the yarn through the closed hole to the inside of the heart and leave it there.***

Second lobe

Rejoin the yarn to the outer stitch at the edge of the heart, ch 1 and work 1 sc (*UKdc*) into each st (20 sts).

There will be a small gap in the sts in the centre of the heart where the two lobes meet. Now is the time to close this up by inserting a few sts using a spare length of yarn and the large-eyed tapestry needle.

Next round: sc (*UKdc*) in each st around (20 sts).

Now stuff the heart, making sure to get the stuffing into the bottom point using your crochet hook or a pencil and filling the completed lobe. For the remaining part of the second lobe, keep adding more stuffing as you go, making sure to pack enough in just before you close the second lobe.

Now follow pattern for first lobe from ** to ***.

CROCUS

Materials:
Small amounts of No. 3 crochet cotton in yellow (A), pale lilac (B) and purple (C); 100g/306yd/280m

Hook:
Size 2.5mm (US B/1, UK 13) crochet hook

Size:
Approx. 4in (10cm) from corner to opposite corner

Stitch note
The picot stitch is worked as follows: work 2 ch, sl st into second ch from hook.

Instructions:

Using yarn A, ch 4 and join with sl st to first ch to form a ring.

Round 1: 3 ch, 11 dc (*UKtr*) in ring, sl st to third ch of initial 3- ch. Fasten off (12 sts).

Round 2: Join B in any st, 3 ch, 1 dc (*UKtr*) in same st, work 2 dc (*UKtr*) in each st around, sl st in third ch of initial 3-ch (24 sts).

Round 3: *3 ch, 1 dc (*UKtr*) in next st, 1 picot, 1 dc (UKtr) in next st, 3 ch, sl st to next st, sl st to next st rep from * 5 times, sl st to last st (6 petals). Fasten off.

Round 4: Join C behind petals to st in between any two petals, *5 ch, sl st to st between next two petals, rep from * to end, sl st to first st.

Round 5: 4 ch [1 dc (*UKtr*) and 1 ch-sp], in next loop work *3 dc (*UKtr*), 2 ch, 3 dc (*UKtr*), 1 ch* rep from * to end, sl st in third ch of initial 3-ch.

Round 6: 3 ch, 2 dc (*UKtr*) in sp, 1 ch, *work [3 dc (*UKtr*), 2 ch, 3 dc (*UKtr*), 1 ch] in corner sp, 3 dc (*UKtr*) in next sp, rep from * to last sp, work [3 dc (*UKtr*), 2 ch, 3 dc (*UKtr*)] in last loop to end, sl st in third ch of 3-ch.

Making up
Fasten off and weave in all loose ends.

Block to achieve correct hexagonal shape and shape petals when wet so that they curve upwards slightly.

These little crocuses are also very attractive and decorative without the edging. This motif would make a lovely shoulder bag.

EVIE PURSE

Materials:

1 ball of worsted yarn (light aran) in walnut (A); 50g/115yd/105m

1 ball of lace weight (2-ply) mohair/silk blend yarn in white (B); 25g/229yd/210m

1 ball of lace weight (2-ply) alpaca/merino blend yarn in white (C), 50g/437yd/400m

Hook:

4mm (US G/6, UK 8) crochet hook

Notions:

5 x large assorted beads

1 x 6¾in (17cm) purse clasp

Size:

Approx. 4 x 6¾in (10 x 17cm)

Instructions:

Using yarn A, make 30 ch.

Row 1: 1 hdc (*UKhtr*) in third ch from hook, 1 hdc (*UKhtr*) in every ch to end (28 sts).

Row 2: 2 ch, 1 hdc (*UKhtr*) in every st to end.

Repeat row 2 until work measures 8in (20cm).

Fasten off yarn.

Flowers (make 5)

With yarns B and C held together and 4mm (US G/6, UK 8) crochet hook, make 5 ch, join with sl st to first ch to form a ring.

Round 1: 5 ch (counts as 1 dc (*UKtr*) and 2 ch), 1 dc (*UKtr*) into ring, [2 ch, 1 dc (*UKtr*) into ring] five times, 2 ch, sl st to third ch of 5-ch at beg of round.

Round 2: [1 hdc (*UKhtr*), 2 dc (*UKtr*), 1 hdc (*UKhtr*), sl st to next dc (*UKtr*)] into every 2-ch space.

Fasten off yarn.

Making up

Press the main piece of the purse gently with an iron, then fold it in half so the RS is facing you. Using the photograph as a guide, sew the flowers to the right side of the purse and sew the beads to the flower centres. Then attach the clasp to the purse. Using mattress stitch, join together the side openings below the clasp on both sides. Attach a lining to the inside if desired.

FLORAL RING

Materials:

Small amounts of No. 3 crochet cotton in
  yellow (A), purple (B), cerise (C) and pink (D);
  100g/306yd/280m
Small piece of matching cotton fabric
Small amount of toy stuffing
Sewing thread to match yarn

Tools:

Size 3mm (US D, UK 10) crochet hook
Sewing needle

Size:

4¼in (11cm) diameter

Instructions:

Using A, make 12 ch, join into a ring with a sl st.

Round 1: work 3 ch, 31 dc (*UKtr*) into ring, join with a sl
st to beg of round [32 dc (*UKtr*)]. Break A.

Round 2: using B, work 4 ch, 2 dc (*UKtr*) into 3rd ch from
hook, *skip 1 dc (*UKtr*), 1 tr (*UKdtr*) into next ch, 2 dc
(*UKtr*) into centre of tr (*UKdtr*)*, rep from * to * fourteen
more times, join to top of 4 ch. Break B.

Round 3: using C, work 3 ch, 1 dc (*UKtr*) into each of the
next 2 dc (*UKtr*), keeping the last loop of each dc (*UKtr*)
on the hook (3 loops on hook), yrh, draw yarn through
all 3 loops, *work 4 ch, 1 dc (*UKtr*) into each of next 3
dc (*UKtr*), keeping the last loop of each dc (*UKtr*) on the
hook, yrh, draw yarn through all loops on hook*, rep
from * to * all round, ending with 4 ch, join to top of first
dc (*UKtr*) in round. Break C.

Round 4: using D, work 1 ch, 4 sc (*UKdc*) into next sp, 1
sc (*UKdc*) into top of cluster, 3 ch, sl st into 3rd ch from
hook, *4 sc (*UKdc*) into next sp, 1 sc (*UKdc*) into top of
next cluster, 3 ch, sl st into 3rd ch from hook*, rep from
* to * all round, join with a sl st to beg of round.
Fasten off and work in all loose ends.

To make the pincushion

Make two motifs. Using a motif as a template, cut two
circles of fabric slightly bigger than the motif, thus
leaving enough fabric to form the seam. With wrong
sides of the fabric facing, sew a seam by hand or on
a sewing machine all round the circle, leaving a small
opening to turn and stuff the pincushion. Turn the
fabric lining right side out and press lightly to form a
neat circle. Stuff the cushion firmly and then close the
opening with a few concealed stitches. Place the two
motifs together and join them by sewing the tips of the
picots together all round the motif. Leave a gap and
slip the cushion into the crocheted cover. Arrange the
cushion neatly then close up the gap.

FLIRTY FLOWERS HAT

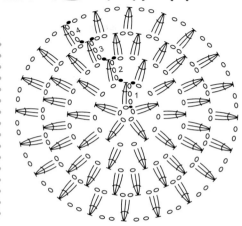

Materials:

2 x balls of aran/bulky (chunky) weight multicoloured yarn in wine; 50g/131yd/120m

Hooks:

Sizes 6mm (US J/10, UK 4) and 7mm (US K/10½, UK 2) crochet hooks

Size:

Head circumference 54–58cm (21¼–23in)

Gauge (tension) sample

4 pattern repeats and 5 rounds using the 7mm (US L/11, UK 2) crochet hook = 4 x 4in (10 x 10cm).
Change your hook if necessary to obtain the correct gauge (tension).

Basic design

Work in rounds following the crochet chart. Start every round with 3 ch instead of the 1st dc (*UKtr*) and join up into a round with a sl st into the 3rd ch from the start of the round. The numbers on the chart show the round transition. Rounds 1–4 are shown in full. After this, rep round 4 until the required length is achieved.

Instructions:

Start the beanie at the crown and work in rounds down to the bottom edge.

Using the 7mm (US L/11, UK 2) crochet hook, begin with 5 ch and join into a ring with a sl st.

Rounds 1–4: Follow the chart, working the clusters of 3 dc (*UKtr*) in the first round into the centre of the ring.

Rounds 5–12: Rep round 4.

Round 13: 1 ch, * 2 sc (*UKdc*) around the next 2 ch of the previous round * , rep from * to * all around. Close up the round with a sl st (40 sts).

Rounds 14–17: Start each round with 1 ch, then work sc (*UKdc*) into each st around; join with a sl st.

Small flowers

Once you have made the hat, cut off the yarn at the point where the colour corresponds to that required for the flower centre (pink in the example below).

Using the 6mm (US J/10, UK 4) hook, 5 ch and join into a ring with sl st.

Round 1 (pink centre): Work round 1 of the crochet chart.

Round 2 (deep pink petals): Cut the yarn and find a length in the colour you want for the petals. For each petal, work under a 2-ch of the previous round: * 1 sc (*UKdc*), 2 ch, cluster of 3 dc (*UKtr*), 2 ch, 1 sc (*UKdc*) *, rep from * to * another four times. Close up the round with a sl st.

Large flowers

Use yarn from the ball in the required colour.

Using the 6mm (US J/10, UK 4) hook, 5 ch in purple or deep pink and join into a ring with a sl st.

Round 1 (in purple or deep pink): Work round 1 of the crochet chart.

Round 2 (in red or purple): For each petal, work under a 2-ch of the previous round: * 1 sc (*UKdc*), 2 ch, 4 dc (*UKtr*), 2 ch, 1 sc (*UKdc*) * , rep from * to * another four times. Close up the round with a sl st.

Making up

Make three flowers in total and sew on to the side of the beanie, using the photograph as a guide.

WISHING STAR

Materials:

1 ball of No. 5 crochet cotton in white
  (this is sufficient to make several stars);
  100g/437yd/400m

Small amount of metallic silver yarn

20in (0.5m) of narrow white ribbon

1 large sparkly button

White sewing thread

Tools:

Size 2mm (US B/1, UK 14) crochet hook

Sewing needle

Size:

Approx. 3¼in (8cm) in diameter

Instructions:

Using white crochet cotton, make 6 ch then join with a sl st into a ring.

Round 1: 1 ch, work 12 sc (*UKdc*) into the ring then join with sl st to first ch.

Round 2: 5 ch, skip 1 sc (*UKdc*), sc (*UKdc*) into next sc (*UKdc*), all around, join to 1st of 5 ch at beg of round [6 x 5-ch loops].

Round 3: sl st into first 5 ch loop, 2 ch, work 5 dc (*UKtr*) into same loop, 1 sc (*UKdc*) in next sc (*UKdc*). *6 dc (*UKtr*) into 5 ch loop, 1 sc (*UKdc*) into next sc (*UKdc*),* repeat from * to * four times more and then join with a sl st to beg of round.

Round 4: sl st to 2nd dc (*UKtr*), 2 ch, 1 dc (*UKtr*) into same dc (*UKtr*), 2 dc (*UKtr*) into each of next 3 dc (*UKtr*), 1 sc (*UKdc*) into next sc (*UKdc*), *skip next dc (*UKtr*), 2 dc (*UKtr*) into each of next 4 dc (*UKtr*), skip 1 dc (*UKtr*), 1 sc (*UKdc*) into sc (*UKdc*),* repeat from * to * four times more and then join with a sl st to beg of round. Break off white.

Round 5: join in metallic yarn to same place as sl st and proceed as follows. Work *1 sc (*UKdc*) into each of the next 4 dc (*UKtr*), **4 ch, sl st into 3rd ch from hook (1 picot formed), ** repeat from ** to ** twice more, 1 sc (*UKdc*) into each of the next 4 dc (*UKtr*), 1 sc (*UKdc*) into sc (*UKdc*) of row 4, thus pulling up a long loop,* repeat from * to * five times more and then join with a sl st to beg of round. Fasten off.

Making up
Using white thread, stitch the large sparkly button to the centre front of the star. Thread the ribbon through the top of one point to make a hanging loop. Decide how long you want the ribbon loop to be and trim the ribbon as necessary. Either tie the ends of the ribbon together in a knot or stitch them to form a loop.

PASSION FLOWER

Materials:

Small amounts of No. 3 crochet cotton in cream and pale green; 100g/306yd/280m

Fluffy yarn in blue/black

Small amounts of light worsted (DK/8-ply) yarn in lime green and purple

Sewing thread

Tools:

Size 3mm (US D, UK 10) crochet hook

Sewing needle

Instructions:

Petals

Work from the centre of the flower outwards.

Using cream crochet cotton, make an adjustable ring (see page 21).

2 ch, 6 sc (UKdc) into ring, pull to close, sl st into top ch of 2 ch.

Round 1: 1 ch, 1 sc (UKdc) into base sc (UKdc), 2 sc (UKdc) into each of next 7 ch, sl st into 1 ch.

Round 2: 1 ch,1 sc (UKdc), *2 sc (UKdc), 1 sc (UKdc), 1 sc (UKdc)*, repeat from * to * four more times, 1 sc (UKdc), sl st into 1 ch.

Round 3: 1 ch, *2 sc (UKdc) into next sc (UKdc), 1 sc (UKdc) into next sc (UKdc)*, repeat from * to * nine more times.

Join in the pale green crochet cotton and sl st into 1 ch. Fasten off the cream cotton.

Using the pale green cotton, *10 ch, skip 2 ch, dc (UKtr) into next 4 ch, hdc (UKhtr) into next 4 ch, sl st into next sc (UKdc) of round 4, turn, sl st into next 8 ch, sc (UKdc) into 2 ch sp, turn, dc (UKtr) into next 4 ch, hdc (UKhtr) into next 4 ch, sl st into next sc (UKdc) from round 3, sl st into next sc (UKdc)*, repeat from * to * nine more times. Fasten off.

Join the fluffy yarn at the base of petal 1, *3 ch, sl st into base of next petal*, repeat from * to * nine more times. Fasten off.

Flower centre

With lime green yarn, 4 ch, sl st into ring, sc (UKdc) into ring, 4 ch, skip 1 ch, hdc (UKhtr) into next ch, sl st into next ch twice, sl st into ring, *3 ch, skip 1 ch, hdc (UKhtr) into next ch, sl st into next ch, sl st into ring*, repeat from * to * three more times. Fasten off.

With purple yarn, 3 ch, skip 1 ch, 1 hdc (UKhtr), 1 sl st. Place this in the middle of the lime green flower centre and sew it in place securely. Sew the flower centre to the middle of the passion flower.

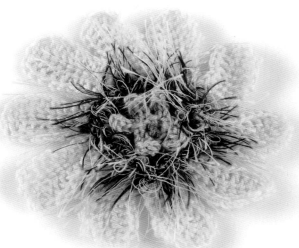

This stunning creation looks fabulous on clothes, bags and accessories.

BELINDA BUTTERFLY BEAR

Materials:

1 ball of No. 5 crochet cotton in white and small
amounts in beige, dark brown and light blue;
100g/437yd/400m

Black and yellow floss for embroidering features
and butterfly

Tiny paper flowers in yellow and pink

Tiny pale blue ribbon bow

Toy stuffing

Sewing threads to match crochet cotton

Tools:

Size 2.5mm (US B/1, UK 13) crochet hook

Sewing needle

Instructions:

Make the bear following the basic instructions on page
37, using white for the head, body, arms and legs and
beige for the muzzle and ears.

Skirt

Row 1: using light blue, make 30 ch, join with a sl st
to beg of row, making sure you do not twist the chain.

Row 2: 1 ch, 1 sc (*UKdc*) in each ch to end, joining
as before.

Row 3: 4 ch, skip 2 sc (*UKdc*), 1 sc (*UKdc*) in next sc
(*UKdc*), *2 ch, skip 2 ch, 1 sc (*UKdc*) in next sc (UKdc)*,
rep from * to * all round, 2 ch, sl st to 2nd of 4 turning
ch of previous row.

Row 4: *3 ch, 1 sc (*UKdc*) in next 3 ch loop*, rep from *
to * all round, joining as before.

Row 5: as row 4.

Row 6: [1 sc (*UKdc*), 2 dc (*UKtr*), 1 sc (*UKdc*)] in each
3-ch loop. Join with a sl st to beg of row. Fasten off.

Basket

Row 1: using dark brown, make 3 ch, 14 dc (*UKtr*) in 2nd
ch from hook, join with a sl st.

Row 2: 2 dc (*UKtr*) in each dc (*UKtr*) all round. Join
as before.

Row 3: working into back loop of stitch only, 1 dc (*UKtr*)
in each st to end, join as before.

Work 2 rows of sc (*UKdc*). Fasten off.

Basket handle

Using dark brown, make 20 ch, 1 sc (*UKdc*) in 2nd ch
from hook, 1 sc (*UKdc*) in each ch to end. Fasten off.

Butterfly

Using light blue, make 2 ch, 3 dc (*UKtr*) in 2nd ch from
hook, 1 sl st in same place, 3 ch, 3 dc (*UKtr*) in same
place, 1 sl st in same place, 3 ch, 3 dc (*UKtr*) in same
place, sl st in same place, 3 ch, 3 dc (*UKtr*) in same
place, sl st in same place and fasten off. Sew the centre
together to form four wings.

Making up

Work in the ends on all the pieces. Attach the tiny blue
ribbon bow to the bear's head. Slip the skirt on to the
bear with the join at the centre back. Add a tiny amount
of stuffing to the basket to give it a rounded shape and
sew one end of the handle on to each side. Wire the
flowers together into a neat bunch, place them inside
the basket and secure them with a few stitches. Shape
the butterfly's wings, then take some yellow floss and
sew a tiny spot on to each wing using French knots. Use
some black floss to work the body in straight stitches.
Fray the end of the black floss to make antennae. Sew
the butterfly to the bear's paw.

VALENTINE

Instructions:

Using yarn A, ch 10, sc (*UKdc*) in second ch from hook to end (9 sts).

Rows 1–9: 1 ch, sc (*UKdc*) to end. This makes a square.

Right lobe

Row 10: 1 ch, 9 tr (*UKdtr*) into centre st of one side of square, sl st to corner.

Left lobe (working along the next straight edge)

Row 11: 1 ch, 9 tr (*UKdtr*) into centre st of next side of square, sl st to corner.

Row 12: sc (*UKdc*) down one edge of the square and up the other side, stopping at the start of the tr (*UKdtr*) sts, sl st to join.

Fasten off.

Row 13: Join yarn B to the middle of the two lobes and sc (*UKdc*) around. Work two sc (*UKdc*) into one st at the centre of each lobe, and into the st at the bottom point, work 1 sc (*UKdc*), 1 hdc (*UKhtr*), 1 sc (*UKdc*); sl st into middle of lobes to finish.

Fasten off and weave in all loose ends.

Materials:

Small amounts of light worsted (DK/8-ply) handknit cotton in red (A) and white (B); 50g/93yd/85m

Tools:

Size 4mm (US G/6, UK 8) crochet hook

Notions:

1 heart-shaped red button

Size:

Approx. 4in (10cm) from bottom point to centre top between lobes

Flower

Using yarn B, ch 4, sl st to first ch to form a ring.

Round 1: 1 ch, sc (*UKdc*) in ring ten times, sl st to ch-1 to join.

Round 2: [2 ch, 2 dc (*UKtr*), 1 hdc (*UKhtr*)] in first st, sl st to next st, *1 hdc (*UKhtr*), 2 dc (UKtr), 1 hdc (*UKhtr*) in next st, sl st in next st, rep from * three times, sl st to first st to join.

Fasten off.

Making up

Position the button centrally over the flower and attach them to the centre of the heart through the button, using yarn A. Fasten off and weave in all loose ends.

BORAGE

Materials:
Small amounts of crochet cotton in ecru (A), mid-blue (B), dark green (C) and pink (D); 100g/306yd/280m

Tools:
Size 2.5mm (US B/1, UK 13) crochet hook

Size:
Approx. 3½in (9cm) from corner to opposite side

Notes
The picot stitch is worked as follows: work 2 ch, sl st into second ch from hook.

Instructions:

Using yarn A, ch 4 and join with sl st to first ch to form a ring.

Round 1: 1 ch, 10 sc (UKdc) in ring, sl st to first ch (10 sts). Fasten off.

Round 2: Attach yarn B to any st, 3 ch, 1 dc (UKtr) in same st, 2 dc (UKtr) in each st around, sl st to third ch of 3-ch (20 sts).

Round 3: *4 ch, [1 tr (UKdtr), 1 picot, 1 tr (UKdtr), 1 dc (UKtr)] in next st, 3 ch, sl st in next 3 sts, rep from * four times to end, sl st to last st. Fasten off.

Round 4: Attach yarn C to middle st between two petals, *6 ch, sl st in second ch from hook, 3 ch, sl st in same st between petals, 4 ch, sl st in middle st between next two petals, rep from * four times. Fasten off.

Round 5: Attach yarn D to a 4-ch loop, [3 ch, 2 dc (UKtr), 2 ch, 3 dc (UKtr), 1 ch] in same loop, in next loop work *[3 dc (UKtr), 2 ch, 3 dc (UKtr), 1 ch], rep from * three times, sl st to third ch of initial 3-ch.

Round 6: sl st to corner sp, [3 ch, 2 dc (UKtr), 2 ch, 3 dc (UKtr), 1 ch] in same sp, *in next ch sp work [3 dc (UKtr), 1 ch], in corner sp work [3 dc (UKtr), 2 ch, 3 dc (UKtr), 1 ch], rep from * three times, 3 dc (UKtr) in last ch sp, 1 ch, sl st to third ch of 3-ch.

Making up
Fasten off and weave in all loose ends. Block to achieve correct pentagon shape and pin petals out to dry flat.

The petals of this flower will kink slightly to the left because of the use of the picot stitch. This gives them a slightly lop-sided charm.

APPLE CHARM PURSE

Instructions:

Make 2 purse motifs

With yarn A and 4mm (US G/6, UK 8) crochet hook, make 5 ch, join with sl st to first st to form a ring.

Round 1: 2 ch (counts as 1 hdc (*UKhtr*)), 9 hdc (UKhtr) into ring, sl st to top of 2 ch (10 sts).

Round 2: 2 ch (counts as 1 hdc (*UKhtr*)), 1 hdc (*UKhtr*) in base of 2 ch, *2 hdc (*UKhtr*) in next st, rep from * to end, sl st to first st (20 sts).**

Round 3: 2 ch (counts as 1 hdc (*UKhtr*)), 2 hdc (*UKhtr*) in next st, *1 hdc (*UKhtr*) in next st, 2 hdc (*UKhtr*) in next st, rep from * to end, sl st to first st (30 sts).

Round 4: sl st in next st, 1 sc (*UKdc*) in next st, [2 hdc (*UKhtr*) in next st] eleven times, 1 sc (*UKdc*) in next st, sl st in next 2 sts, 1 sc (*UKdc*) in next st, [2 hdc (*UKhtr*) in next st] eleven times, 1 sc (*UKdc*) in next st, sl st in next st.

Fasten off.

Apple centre

With yarn B and 4mm (US G/6, UK 8) crochet hook work to ** of back.

Next round: sl st to first st, 1 sc (*UKdc*) in next st, [2 hdc (*UKhtr*) in next st] seven times, 1 sc (*UKdc*) in next st, sl st in next st, 1 sc (*UKdc*) in next st, [2 hdc (*UKhtr*) in next st] seven times, 1 sc (*UKdc*) in next st.

Fasten off yarn.

Leaf

With yarn C and 4mm (US G/6, UK 8) crochet hook, make 8 ch.

Row 1: 1 sc (*UKdc*) into second ch from hook, 1 hdc (*UKhtr*) in next st, 1 dc (*UKtr*) in next st, 1 tr (*UKdtr*) in next st, 1 dc (*UKtr*) in next st, 1 hdc (*UKhtr*) in next st, 1 sc (*UKdc*) in next st.

Stalk and snap hook loop (make 1 of each)

With yarn A or D and 4mm (US G/6, UK 8) crochet hook, make 7 ch.

Row 1: 1 sc (*UKdc*) in second ch from hook, 1 sc (*UKdc*) in every ch to end.

Fasten off yarn.

Making up

Sew the beads to the white centre of the apple, then attach the apple centre to the front. Sew the leaf and stalk to the top curve of the apple. Feed the snap hook through the loop and sew the loop onto the side of the purse. With RS together and using mattress stitch, sew the back and front pieces of the apple together leaving a 1½in (4cm) opening on the left side. Turn through and sew the snap fastener to the inside edges of the opening.

CIRCLE & SHELL SQUARE

Materials:

Small amounts of No. 3 crochet cotton in claret (A), white (B) and pink (C); 100g/306yd/280m

Hook:

Size 3mm (US D, UK 10) crochet hook

Size:

2in (5cm) diameter

Instructions:

Using A, make 7 ch, join into a circle with a sl st.

Round 1: 3 ch, work 15 dc (UKtr) into circle, join with a sl st to top of 3 ch at beg of round. Fasten off yarn A.

Round 2: using B, 4 ch, skip 1 dc (UKtr), *7 dc (UKtr) into next dc (UKtr), 1 ch, skip 1 dc (UKtr), 1 dc (UKtr) into next dc (UKtr), 1 ch, skip 1 dc (UKtr)*, rep from * to * twice more, ending last rep with 7 dc (UKtr) into next dc (UKtr), 1 ch, skip 1 dc (UKtr), sl st into 3rd of 4 ch at beg of round. Fasten off yarn B.

Round 3: using C, *1 sc (UKdc) into next sp, 1 sc (UKdc) into each of next 3 dc (UKtr), 3 dc (UKtr) into next dc (UKtr) [at the corner], 1 sc (UKdc) into each of next 3 dc (UKtr), 1 sc (UKdc) into next sp, 1 sc (UKdc) into next dc (UKtr)*, rep from * to * all round, join with a sl st to beg of round. Fasten off and weave in all loose ends.

LIGHT AND LACY HAT

Materials:

1 ball of lace weight (2-ply) mohair/silk blend yarn in steel grey; 25g/229yd/210m

1 ball of fine metallic crochet thread in silver; 25g/109yd/100m

Hook:

Size 4mm (US G/6, UK 8) crochet hook

Size:

Head circumference 21¼–23in (54–58cm)

Gauge (tension) sample

15 dc (*UKtr*), i.e. 3 shells of the basic pattern, and 8 rows using the 4mm (US G/6, UK8) crochet hook = 4 x 4in (10 x 10cm). Change your hook if necessary to obtain the correct gauge (tension).

Tip

Adjust the size of the hat band to obtain the perfect fit. Work the band using a 5mm (US H/8, UK 6) crochet hook for a larger head or a 3.5mm (US E/4, UK 9) hook for a smaller head.

Basic pattern

The pattern is worked in rows following the chart. It is worked over multiples of 4 sts (including 1 extra ch and 3 turning ch). The numbers on each side of the chart show the start of the row each time. Replace the 1st dc (*UKtr*) of each row with 3 ch. Always sl st the last dc (*UKtr*) of each row into the 3rd turning ch. Start the row with the st before the pattern repeat, continue crocheting the repeats as required and finish with the st after the repeat. Work rows 1–5 then rep rows 2–5 three times.

Note

For 1 shell, work 5 dc (*UKtr*) in the same st in the 1st row and in the 3rd and 5th rows always crochet the dcs (*UKtrs*) around the ch of the previous row.

Instructions:

Work the hat as a flat piece, starting at the bottom edge and working up to the point at the top. Join the edges together afterwards to form the centre-back seam.

Using one strand of lace weight mohair/silk yarn and one strand of silver metallic thread together and the 4mm (US G/6, UK 8) hook, begin with 68 ch (includes the 3-ch of the 1st dc/*UKtr*).

Rows 1–5: Work following the chart.

Repeat rows 2–5 three times but on the final row (row 17) start the decreases for the shape of the hat as follows:

Row 17: 3 ch, continue working as for row 5 of the crochet pattern, but * instead of 5 dc (*UKtr*), crochet just 3 dc (*UKtr*) around the 2 ch of the previous row * , rep from * to * another fifteen times. End the row with 1 dc (*UKtr*).

Row 18: * 3 ch, dc3tog (*UKtr3tog*) * , rep from * to * fifteen times, ending the row with 1 dc (*UKtr*) (17 sts).

Row 19: 1 ch, sc (*UKdc*) into each st (17 sts).

Row 20: * 1 ch, sc2tog (*UKdc2tog*) * , rep from * to * seven times.

Making up

Draw together the remaining st using the yarn end, catching in the decrease st. Close up the back seam with a single strand of yarn.

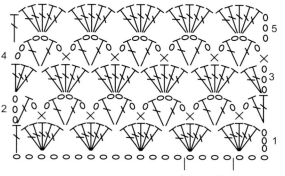

Repeat (4 sts)

CHRISTMAS BELL

Materials:

- 1 ball of No. 5 crochet cotton in white;
  100g/437yd/400m
- 2 burgundy organza ribbon embellishments
- 20in (0.5m) gold-edged burgundy ribbon
- Spray fabric stiffener (starch)
- Craft glue

Hook:

Size 2mm (US B/1, UK 14) crochet hook

Size:

Approx. 2¼in (6cm) high, excluding the ribbon

Instructions:

Using white crochet cotton, make 8 ch then join with a sl st into a ring.

Round 1: work 16 sc (*UKdc*) into the ring then join with a sl st.

Round 2: 6 ch, *skip 1 sc (*UKdc*), 1 dc (*UKtr*) into next sc (*UKdc*), 2 ch,* repeat all around, join to 3rd ch of 6 ch at beg of round.

Round 3: sl st to first 2 ch sp, 3 ch, 2 dc (*UKtr*), 1 ch, 3 dc (*UKtr*) into same space, *1 sc (*UKdc*) into next sp, 3 dc (*UKtr*), 1 ch, 3 dc (*UKtr*) into next sp,* repeat from * to * twice more, 1 sc (*UKdc*) into last sp, join to base of first dc (*UKtr*) of round with a sl st.

Round 4: 5 ch, *4 dc (*UKtr*), 2 ch, 4 dc (*UKtr*) into centre of next group, 1 dc (*UKtr*) into next sc (*UKdc*),* repeat from * to *, ending last repeat with 1 sl st into 3rd ch of 5 ch at the start of the round.

Round 5: 5 ch, *5 dc (*UKtr*), 3 ch, 5 dc (*UKtr*) into centre of next group, 1 dc (*UKtr*) into next dc (*UKtr*),* repeat from * to * ending last repeat with 1 sl st into 3rd ch of 5 ch at start of round.

Round 6: 8 ch, 1 sc (*UKdc*) into centre of next group, *5 ch, 1 dc (*UKtr*) into next dc (*UKtr*), 5 ch, 1 sc (*UKdc*) into centre of next group,* repeat from * to * ending with sl st into 3rd ch of 8-ch made at beg of round.

Round 7: *into next 5 ch sp work [1 sc (*UKdc*), 1 hdc (*UKhtr*), 1 dc (*UKtr*), 1 hdc (*UKhtr*), 1 sc (*UKdc*)], 1 sc (*UKdc*) in next sc (*UKdc*) or dc (*UKtr*),* repeat from * to * all around, join with a sl st.

Round 8: * work 1 sc (*UKdc*) into each sc (*UKdc*) to dc (*UKtr*) at point of each group, 3 ch, sl st into base of st just worked (picot made), * repeat from * to * all around, join with a sl st. Fasten off.

Bell clapper

Using white crochet cotton, make 3 ch, work 10 dc (*UKtr*) into 2nd ch from hook, join with a sl st. Fasten off then run thread through last row, draw up tight into a ball and fasten off. Crochet a chain 2in (5cm) long then fasten off. Attach the ball to the end of the chain firmly.

Making up

Work in all yarn ends on the bell. Spray the bell with fabric stiffener and then stretch it to shape over a suitable container. Leave it to dry. Pull out the picot points as the fabric stiffener dries to give a nice shape. When the bell is dry, attach the clapper inside by threading the chain through the hole at the top of the bell and gluing it in place. Make a loop of ribbon and thread it through the top hole in the bell; glue the ends in place. Attach the two organza flowers on either side.

RETRO DAISY

Materials:
- Small amounts of No. 3 crochet cotton in orange, purple, white, turquoise, yellow and dark green; 100g/306yd/280m
- Sewing thread

Tools:
- Size 3mm (US D, UK 10) crochet hook
- Sewing needle

Instructions:

Orange flower

With orange crochet cotton, 8 ch, sl st into ring.

Round 1: 1 ch, 12 sc (UKdc), join with sl st.

Round 2: 9 ch, sl st into base sc (UKdc), sl st into next ch, sl st into next ch, *10 ch, sl st into next ch, sl st into next ch*, repeat from * to * three more times, 10 ch, sl st to next ch (makes 6 petals).

Round 3: *sl st into centre of first 10 ch, 20 sc (UKdc) along length of ch, sl st into base sc (UKdc)*, repeat from * to * five more times working into the centre of each 10 ch sp.

Cut and tie off the end.

Orange flower centre

Round 1: with purple crochet cotton, make an adjustable ring, 1 ch, 6 sc (UKdc).

Change to white crochet cotton, sl st into 1 ch.

Round 2: 1 ch, 2 hdc (UKhtr) in each sc (UKdc), sl st into 1 ch.

Cut and tie off the ends.

Add a splash of colour to your summer picnic or barbeque with these fun flowers.

Stalk

With dark green crochet cotton, make 20 ch, skip 1 ch, sc (UKdc) down length of ch, 1 sl st across bottom of ch, 20 sc (UKdc) to top of ch.

Fasten off and sew in the ends.

Lay the flower centre in the middle of the orange daisy petals, sew them together securely and fasten off.

Turn the flower over, place the stalk so that the top is in the centre of the daisy petals and sew it in place securely with cotton thread.

Turquoise flower

This is made in the same way as the orange flower, but without the flower centre and stalk.

Yellow flower

With yellow crochet cotton, 6 ch, sl st into ring.

Round 1: 1 ch, 10 sc (UKdc), join with sl st.

Round 2: 7 ch, sl st into base sc (UKdc), sl st into next ch, sl st into next ch, *8 ch, sl st into next ch, sl st into next ch*, repeat from * to * twice more, 8 ch, sl st to next ch (makes 6 petals).

Round 3: *sl st into centre of first 8 ch, 16 sc (UKdc) along length of ch, sl st into base sc (UKdc)*, repeat from * to * five more times working into the centre of each 8 ch sp.

Cut and tie off the end.

Materials:

1 ball each of No. 5 crochet cotton in beige and mid-green, and small amounts in dark brown, mid-brown, light blue and dark green; 100g/437yd/400m

Black floss for embroidering features

Small amount of metallic yarn in silver

2 tiny plastic flowers

Tiny card fork and trowel

Toy stuffing

Sewing threads in colours to match crochet cotton

Tools:

Size 2.5mm (US B/1, UK 13) crochet hook

Sewing needle

ANTHONY GARDEN BEAR

Instructions:

Make the bear following the basic instructions on page 37, using beige for the head, body and arms and dark brown for the muzzle and ears. For the legs, work using mid-green, then join in light blue at row 8 and work rows 8, 10 and 12 in light blue.

Apron

Row 1: using mid-green, make 17 ch, 1 dc (*UKtr*) in 4th ch from hook, 1dc (*UKtr*) in each ch to end, turn.

Row 2: 1 ch, 1 sc (*UKdc*) in each sc (*UKdc*) to end, turn.

Row 3: 3 ch, skip 1 dc (*UKtr*), 1 dc (*UKtr*) in each dc (*UKtr*) to end.

Row 4: 1 ch, 1 sc (*UKdc*) in each dc (*UKtr*) to end, turn.

Rows 5 and 6: rep rows 3 and 4.

Row 7: sl st over 4 dc (*UKtr*), 3 ch, 1 dc (*UKtr*) in each st to last 3 dc (*UKtr*), turn.

Row 8: 3 ch, dc (*UKtr*) 2 tog, work to last 3 sts, dc (*UKtr*) 2 tog, 1 dc (*UKtr*) in top of turning ch of previous row.

Pocket

Row 1: using dark green, make 10 ch, 1 sc (*UKdc*) in 2nd ch from hook, 1 sc (*UKdc*) in each ch to end, turn.

Row 2: 1 ch, 1 sc (*UKdc*) in each sc (*UKdc*) to end, turn.

Rows 3 and 4: rep row 2. Fasten off.

Spade – blade

Row 1: using metallic yarn, make 7 ch, 1 sc (*UKdc*) in 2nd ch from hook, 1 sc (*UKdc*) in each ch to end, turn.

Row 2: 1 ch, 1 sc (*UKdc*) in each sc (*UKdc*) to end, turn.

Repeat last row twelve times. Fasten off.

Spade – shaft

Row 1: using dark brown, make 12 ch, 1 sc (*UKdc*) in 2nd ch from hook, 1 sc (*UKdc*) in each ch to end, turn.

Row 2: 1 ch, 1 sc (*UKdc*) in each sc (*UKdc*) to end, turn.

Row 3: rep row 2. Fasten off.

Spade – handle

Row 1: using dark brown, make 8 ch, 1 sc (*UKdc*) in 2nd ch from hook, 1 sc (*UKdc*) in each ch to end, turn.

Row 2: 1 ch, 1 sc (*UKdc*) in each sc (*UKdc*) to end, turn.

Row 3: rep row 2. Fasten off.

Flowerpot

Row 1: using dark brown, make 2 ch, 6 sc (*UKdc*) in 2nd ch from hook, join in a circle with a sl st.

Row 2: 1 ch, 2 sc (*UKdc*) in each sc (*UKdc*) all round, join as before.

Rows 3–7: 1 ch, 1 sc (*UKdc*) in each st, join as before.

Soil for pot

Using dark brown, make 3 ch, 6 sc (*UKdc*) in 2nd ch from hook, join in a circle. Work 2 sc (*UKdc*) in each st all round, join and fasten off.

Making up

Work in the ends on all the pieces. Sew the pocket to the front of the apron. Using green yarn, make a chain long enough to go round the bear's neck, then attach the top of the apron at each corner. Make two short lengths of chain as ties for the apron and attach one on each side. Put the apron on to the bear and tie the apron at the back. Fold the blade part of the spade in half lengthwise and stitch the sides together. Fold the shaft lengthways into a tight oblong and stitch it firmly. Do the same with the handle. Stitch the handle to the shaft, then attach the shaft to the blade. Lightly stuff the flowerpot to give it shape. Put the soil inside the pot and catch it in place. Push the two plastic flowers through the centre of the soil and secure with a few stitches. Stitch the fork and trowel on to the pocket.

AVA PURSE

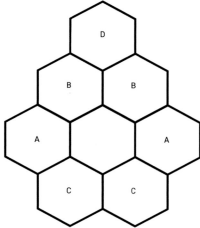

Materials:
1 ball of worsted yarn (UK light aran) in turquoise; 100g/219yd/200m
Fabric for lining (optional)
Stiff iron-on interfacing (optional)

Hook:
4mm (US G/6, UK 8) crochet hook

Notions:
1 x large snap fastener

Size:
Each hexagon is approx. 4in (10cm) wide

Instructions:

Hexagons (make 8)
With 4mm (US G/6, UK 8) crochet hook make 5 ch, join with sl st to form a ring.

Round 1: 4 ch (counts as 1 dc (*UKtr*) and 1 ch), [1 dc (*UKtr*) in ring, 1 ch] eleven times, join with sl st to third ch of 4-ch at beg of round.

Round 2: 3 ch (counts as 1 dc (*UKtr*)), 2 dc (*UKtr*) in next 1-ch sp, 1 dc (*UKtr*) in next dc (*UKtr*), 2 ch, [1 dc (*UKtr*), in next dc (*UKtr*), 2 dc (*UKtr*) in next 1-ch sp, 1 dc (*UKtr*) in next dc (*UKtr*), ch 2] five times, join with sl st to top of beg 3-ch.

Round 3: 3 ch (counts as 1 dc (*UKtr*)), 1 dc (*UKtr*) in base of 3-ch, 1 dc (*UKtr*) in each of next 2 dc (*UKtr*), 2 dc (*UKtr*) in next dc (*UKtr*), 2 ch, [2 dc (*UKtr*) in next dc (*UKtr*), 1 dc (*UKtr*) in each of next 2 dc (*UKtr*), 2 dc (*UKtr*) in next dc (*UKtr*), ch 2] five times, join with sl st to top of beg 3-ch.

Fasten off yarn.

Making up
Press each hexagon gently with an iron and weave in all loose ends. Using the diagram (right) as a guide, join the hexagons together using sc (*UKdc*) on the right side of the work.

Hexagons A form the sides; join to one side of hexagons B and C. Join each A, B and C on one side to the centre hexagon. Join D to each B on one side. Cut approximately 7½ x 13in (19 x 33cm) of fabric and interfacing, leaving ¼in (5mm) for the seam allowance, cut to shape and sew to the inside of the purse.

Sew a snap fastener to the underside of hexagon D and in the middle of the two C hexagons to finish.

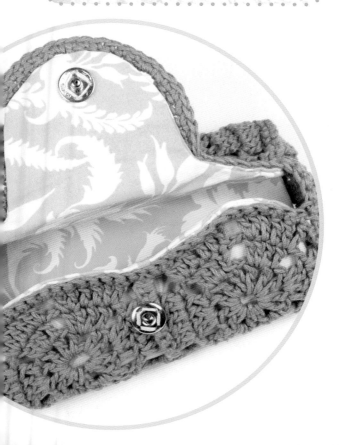

PINWHEEL CIRCLE

Materials:

Small amounts of No. 3 crochet cotton
in white (A), blue (B) and red (C);
100g/306yd/280m

Hook:

Size 3mm (US D, UK 10) crochet hook

Size:

4in (10cm) diameter

Instructions:

Using A, make 10 ch, join with a sl st to form
a ring.

Round 1: , 3 ch, work 31 dc (*UKtr*) into ring,
join with a sl st to 3 ch at beg of round.
Fasten off yarn A.

Round 2: using B, *4 ch, 1 sc (*UKdc*) into 4th
dc (*UKtr*)*, rep all round, joining last rep to
base of 4 ch at
beg of round.

Round 3: using B, sl st into first sp, 4 ch, 5
dc (*UKtr*) into first sp, *1 ch, 6 dc (*UKtr*) into
next sp*, rep from * to * all round, join last rep
to top of 4 ch at beg of round. Fasten off yarn B.

Round 4: using C, *6 ch, 1 sc (*UKdc*) into sp
between groups*, rep from * to * all round, join
to top of 6 ch at beg of round.

Round 5: using C, sl st into first 6 ch sp, 3 ch,
5 dc (*UKtr*), 3 ch, 6 dc (*UKtr*) into next 6 ch sp,
*1 ch, 6 dc (*UKtr*) into next 6 ch sp, 1 ch, [6 dc
(*UKtr*), 3 ch, 6 dc (*UKtr*)] into next sp*, rep from
* to * twice more, 1 ch, 6 dc (*UKtr*) into next 6
ch sp, 1 ch, sl st to top of 3 ch at beg of round.
Fasten off and weave in all loose ends.

MAKING WAVES BEANIE

Materials:

1 ball each of super bulky (super chunky) alpaca/
acrylic blend easy-care yarn in purple, petrol blue,
pine green and indigo; 50g/66yd/60m

Hook:

6mm (US J/10, UK 4) crochet hook

Size:

Head circumference 21¼–23in (54–58cm)

Gauge (tension) sample

1 repeat and 5 rows in the wave pattern using the 6mm
(US J/10, UK4) crochet hook = 3¼ x 4in (8 x 10cm).
Change your hook if necessary to obtain the correct
gauge (tension).

Wave design

The hat is worked in rows following the pattern shown in
the chart. The pattern can be worked over a multiple of 6
sts + 2 (including the turning ch). The numbers on each
side show the start of each row. Start each row with
the number of ch as indicated according to the st height.
Work the 1st hdc (UKhtr) into the 3rd ch from the hook.
Always sl st the last st of each row into the last turning
ch of the previous row. Start the row with the st before
the repeat, work the repeats as required and finish with
the st after the repeat. Work rows 1–5 then work rows
2–4 again (8 rows).

Changing colours

Work in the following colour order: purple, petrol blue,
pine green and indigo. Change colour for each new row
and repeat the colour order as required.

NB: When changing colour, the new colour should be
introduced on the last loop of the st just before the st
that will be made in the new colour to give a perfect
colour transition. In this case, it should be introduced on
the last st of each round.

Instructions:

Work the hat as a flat piece in rows, starting at the
bottom edge and working up to the point at the top.
Join the edges together afterwards to form the
centre-back seam.

Using purple yarn, begin with 50 ch (includes the 1-ch
turning ch).

Rows 1–5: Work following the chart.

Rows 6–8: Rep rows 2–4.

Now decrease to shape the top of the beanie as follows:

Row 9 (purple): 3 ch, dc2tog (UKtr2tog) twenty-four
times and end with 1 dc (UKtr) (25 sts).

Row 10 (petrol blue): 3 ch, dc2tog (UKtr2tog) twelve
times and end with 1 dc (UKtr) (13 sts).

Row 11 (pine green): 1 ch, sc (UKdc) into each st in the
previous row (13 sts).

Draw the remaining sts together with the yarn end,
catching in the decrease st each time.

Making up

For the hat band, work along the foundation-ch edge,
using indigo yarn to work 1 ch, then sc (UKdc) into each
of the 49 sts around. Work 2 rows of sc (UKdc) into
each st. Join side edges to create centre-back seam.

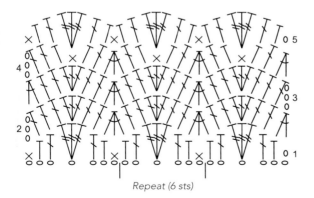

Repeat (6 sts)

Materials:

1 ball each of No. 5 crochet cotton in white and mid-blue plus small amounts of black, red, and orange; 100g/437yd/400m

Small amount of silver metallic yarn

A few small white beads

Small wooden Christmas-tree embellishment, approx. 1½in (4cm) high

Craft glue

Magnetic photo paper

Tools:

Size 2mm (US B/1, UK 14) crochet hook

Embroidery needle

Size:

Approx. 3½in (8cm) square

SNOWY FRIDGE MAGNET

Instructions:

Background

Using white crochet cotton, make 20 ch.

Row 1: work 1 sc (*UKdc*) into 2nd ch from hook, 1 sc (*UKdc*) into each ch to end, turn.

Row 2: 1 ch, work 1 sc (*UKdc*) into each ch to end, turn.

Rows 3–8: repeat row 2.

Change to mid-blue and work 14 rows in sc (*UKdc*). Fasten off.

Join mid-blue to any corner of the background crochet. Work 1 round of sc (*UKdc*) all around the piece, working into row ends or stitches; work 3 sc (*UKdc*) into each corner to keep the work flat. Break mid-blue and join in silver to work a further round of sc (*UKdc*), treating the corners as before; join to beg with a sl st. Fasten off.

Snowman's head

Using white crochet cotton, make 6 ch then join with a sl st to form a tight ring.

Round 1: work 1 sc (*UKdc*) into each ch to end and then join with a sl st.

Round 2: 1 ch, work 2 sc (*UKdc*) into each sc (*UKdc*) to end and then join as before.
Fasten off.

Snowman's body

Using white crochet cotton, make 6 ch then join with a sl st to form a tight ring.

Round 1: work 1 sc (*UKdc*) into each ch to end, join with a sl st.

Round 2: 1 ch, work 2 sc (*UKdc*) into each sc (*UKdc*) to end, join as before.

Round 3: 1 ch, work *1 sc (*UKdc*) into next sc (*UKdc*), 2 sc (*UKdc*) into next sc (*UKdc*),* repeat from * to * all around, join with a sl st.

Round 4: 1 ch, work *1 sc (*UKdc*) into each of next 2 sc (*UKdc*), 2 sc (*UKdc*) into next sc (*UKdc*),* repeat from * to * all around, join with a sl st. Fasten off.

Snowman's scarf

Using red crochet cotton, make 30 ch and then fasten off.

Snowman's hat

Using black crochet cotton, make 7 ch.

Row 1: 1 ch, work 1 sc (*UKdc*) into each ch to end, turn.

Row 2: *sl st over 2 sc (*UKdc*),* repeat from * to * to last 2 sc (*UKdc*), turn.

Rows 3–4: work each st in sc (*UKdc*).

Fasten off.

Making up

Cut a piece of magnetic photo paper the same size as the crocheted background. Using craft glue, stick the paper on to the back of the crocheted background. Press down firmly and allow it to adhere. Sew the snowman's head to his body with a few stitches. Wrap the scarf around his neck and secure. Embroider tiny black dots for eyes and an orange nose. Glue the hat in place on the snowman's head. Stick the snowman on to one side of the background and the tree on to the other, using the photograph as a guide. Glue tiny white beads on to the blue area of the background to suggest falling snow.

CARNATION

Materials:

Small amounts of No. 3 crochet cotton in
red and pink; 100g/306yd/280m

Sewing thread

Tools:

Size 3mm (US D, UK 10)

Sewing needle

Instructions:

With red crochet cotton, make 31 ch.

Row 1: skip 1 ch, 2 dc (*UKtr*) into each ch, 1 ch, turn.

Row 2: 2 hdc (*UKhtr*) into each ch, 1 ch, turn. Fasten off
the red yarn and join in the pink.

Row 3: *3 ch into next ch, ss into next ch*, repeat from
* to * to end of row.

Tie off the end, but leave a good length. Draw this length
through the base chain in a loose gathering stitch. Pull
up the work, tease the flowers into shape and pull the
yarn through the petals to secure.

*For a more subtle effect, the carnation can be worked in
a single colour, as shown by the pale green version in the
photograph opposite.*

Small flower

To make a smaller flower you will need no. 1 crochet
cotton in red and a size 2.5mm (US B/1, UK 13) crochet
hook. Here I have made a pretty ring by attaching the
flower to a ring base using fabric glue.

Make 25 ch.

Row 1: skip 2 ch, 2 sc (*UKdc*) into each ch to end, turn.

Row 2: skip ch, 2 sc (*UKdc*) into each sc (*UKdc*) from
row 1.

Row 3: skip ch, 2 hdc (*UKhtr*) into each sc (*UKdc*) from
row 2 to last 10 sc (*UKdc*), 1 sc (*UKdc*) to end, 1 sc
(*UKdc*) three times in side sts to beginning.

Tie off the end, leaving a length of yarn around 6in
(15cm) long. Use the thread to sew loose gathering
stitches through the base chain. Pull up the work and
form it into a circle. Sew the sides together securely.

Materials:

1 ball each of No. 5 crochet cotton in pale yellow and light blue, and small amounts in mid-brown, dark brown, beige, navy blue and white; 100g/437yd/400m

Dark brown floss for embroidering features, and green and yellow floss for embroidery on easel

Tiny coloured beads for paint palette

6 cocktail sticks, 5 with one blunt end and 1 with two blunt ends

Toy stuffing

Sewing threads in colours to match crochet cotton

Tools:

Size 2.5mm (US B/1, UK 13) crochet hook

Sewing needle

Instructions:

Make the bear following the instructions on page 37, using pale yellow for the head, body, arms and legs, dark brown for the ears and beige for the muzzle.

Sleeves (make 2)

Row 1: using light blue, make 17 ch, 1 dc (*UKtr*) in 3rd ch from hook, 1 dc (*UKtr*) in each ch to end, turn.

Row 2: 3 ch, skip 1 st, 1 dc (*UKtr*) in each st to end.

Rows 3 and 4: rep row 2.

Row 5: 1 ch, 1 sc (*UKdc*) in each st to end. Fasten off.

ROZ THE ARTIST BEAR

Smock (make 2)

Row 1: using light blue, make 20 ch, 1 dc (*UKtr*) in 3rd ch from hook, 1 dc (*UKtr*) in each ch to end, turn.

Row 2: 3 ch, skip 1 st, 1 dc (*UKtr*) in each dc (*UKtr*) to end.

Row 3: 3 ch, skip 1 st, dc (*UKtr*) 2 tog, dc (*UKtr*) to last 3 sts, dc (*UKtr*) 2 tog. 1 dc (*UKtr*) in last st.

Row 4: sl st across next 4 dc (*UKtr*), 3 ch, 1 dc (*UKtr*) in each dc (*UKtr*) to last 3 dc (*UKtr*), turn.

Row 5: 3 ch, 1 dc (*UKtr*) in each st to end.

Row 6: 3 ch, 1 dc (*UKtr*), 1 hdc (*UKhtr*), 5 sc (*UKdc*), 1hdc (*UKhtr*), 2 dc (*UKtr*). Fasten off.

Beret

Row 1: using navy blue, make 30 ch, 1 sc (*UKdc*) in 2nd ch from hook, 1 sc (*UKdc*) in each ch to end, join with a sl st into a circle.

Rows 2 and 3: sc (*UKdc*) all round, join as before.

Row 4: 1 ch, *1 sc (*UKdc*) in next sc (*UKdc*), 2 sc (*UKdc*) in next sc (*UKdc*)*, rep from * to * all round, join as before.

Rows 5 and 6: sc (*UKdc*) all round, join as before.

Row 7: 1 ch, *sc (*UKdc*) 2 tog, 1 sc (*UKdc*) in next st*, rep from * to * all round, ending last rep sc (*UKdc*) 2 tog, join as before.

Row 8: sc (*UKdc*) all round.

Row 9: 1 ch, *sc (*UKdc*) 2 tog, 1 sc (UKdc) in next st*, rep from * to * all round, ending last rep sc (*UKdc*) 2 tog, join as before.

Row 10: sc (*UKdc*) all round.

Row 11: 1 ch, *sc (*UKdc*) 2 tog, 1 sc (*UKdc*) in next st*, rep from * to * all round, ending last rep 1 sc (*UKdc*) in each of last 2 sts, join as before.

Row 12: sc (*UKdc*) all round.

Break yarn and run the thread through each sc (*UKdc*) all round. Draw up and fasten off. Make a tiny loop and attach to the top of the beret.

Easel

Using mid-brown, make a ch the same length as a cocktail stick.

Work 3 rows of sc (*UKdc*) on this chain, fasten off. Wrap the crochet piece lengthways around the stick and oversew it in place firmly. The point should be visible at one end. Repeat this on a further three cocktail sticks, including the one with two blunt ends.

Canvas

Row 1: using white, make 15 ch, 1 sc (*UKdc*) in 2nd ch from hook, 1 sc (*UKdc*) in each ch to end, turn.

Rows 2–14: 1 ch, 1 sc (*UKdc*) in each ch to end, turn.

Fasten off.

Embroider a flower on to the front of the canvas using yellow and green floss.

Palette

Row 1: using white, make 9 ch, 1 sc (*UKdc*) in 2nd ch from hook, 1 sc (*UKdc*) in each ch to end, turn.

Rows 2–6: 1 ch, 1 sc (*UKdc*) in each ch to end.

Do not fasten off but continue along 1 short end as follows:

Row 7: 1 sc (*UKdc*) in next 2 row ends, 2 ch, skip 2 row ends, 1 sc (*UKdc*) in last 2 row ends, turn.

Row 8: 1 ch, sc (*UKdc*) to end, working 2 sc (*UKdc*) in space made on previous row. Fasten off.

Take 8 different coloured beads and sew in place on the palette to represent paint colours.

Making up

Work in the ends on all the pieces. Catch the back and front smock pieces at the shoulder edges, just enough to hold them together. Stitch the sleeves in place. Sew the side and sleeve seams. Put the smock on to the bear and sew the shoulder seams on either side. Place the beret on the side of the bear's head and secure with a few stitches.

Place the palette on the bear's paw and stitch it in place. Take two cocktail sticks and flatten the sharp end of each slightly to split the wood and create a brush effect. Place the brushes into the thumb hole on the palette and secure with some tiny stitches.

Now assemble the easel. First make an A frame by stitching together the top part of two sticks, then sew the stick with two blunt ends horizontally across the centre to create the 'A'. Secure a fourth stick at the back of the frame so that the easel will stand up. Oversew the top of the three upright sticks together firmly. Place the canvas centrally on to the cross bar of the easel and sew it in place.

MYRTLE

Materials:

- 1 ball of light worsted (DK/8-ply) yarn in black; 50g/142yd/130m
- 2 x oval pieces of 6¼ x 6½in (15 x 16cm) lining fabric

Hook:

- 3.75mm (US F/5, UK 9) crochet hook

Notions:

- 1 x rounded purse clasp approx. 4¾in (12cm) wide

Size:

Approx. 6in (15cm) wide and 5½in (14cm) high

Special abbreviations:

dc3tog (UKtr3tog) – dc (UKtr) 3 together cluster: [yrh and insert into st, yrh and draw a loop through, yrh and draw through first 2 loops on hook], rep twice more all in the same st, yrh and draw a loop through all 4 loops on hook.

dc4tog (UKtr4tog) – dc (UKtr) 4 together cluster: [yrh and insert into st, yrh and draw a loop through, yrh and draw through first 2 loops on hook], rep three times more all in the same st, yrh and draw a loop through all 5 loops on hook.

Instructions:

Make 2 purse motifs

With 3.75mm (US F/5) crochet hook make 6 ch, sl st to first ch to form a ring.

Round 1: 1 ch, work 11 sc (UKdc) into ring, sl st to first st.

Round 2: 6 ch (counts as 1 dc (UKtr) and 3 ch), *1 dc (UKtr) in next st, 3 ch, rep from * to end, sl st to top of 3-ch at beg of round (11 dc (UKtr)).

Round 3: 3 ch (counts as 1 dc (UKtr)), dc3tog (UKtr3tog) in next 3-ch sp, 4 ch, *dc4tog (UKtr4tog) in next 3-ch sp, 4 ch, rep from * until all spaces have been worked, sl st to first 3-dc (UKtr) cluster (11 clusters).

Round 4: 1 ch, *5 sc (UKdc) in next 4-ch sp, 1 sc (UKdc) in top of next cluster, rep from * until all spaces have been worked, sl st to first st.

Round 5: 1 ch, sl st into next 2 sts, 3 ch (counts as 1 dc (UKtr)), *7 ch, skip next 5 sts, 1 dc (UKtr) in next st, rep from * ten times more, sl st to first st.

Round 6: 1 ch, *8 sc (UKdc) in next 7-ch sp, 1 sc (UKdc) in top of 1 dc (UKtr), rep from * to end.

Round 7: 1 ch, 1 sc (UKdc) in every st to end, sl st to first st, turn.

Row 8: 1 ch, 1 sc (UKdc) in next 63 sts.

Fasten off yarn.

Making up

With RS facing and using mattress stitch, join the front and back together by sewing all along the raised part. Turn through. This leaves a gap of approximately 6¾in (17cm) to attach to the clasp. Sew in the lining, leaving a ¼in (1cm) seam allowance.

DOG ROSE TRIANGLE

Materials:

Small amounts of No. 3 crochet cotton in
  pale yellow (A), claret (B) and yellow (C);
  100g/306yd/280m

For the mat:

Small amounts of No. 3 crochet cotton in a variety
  of colours, including light and dark green

Hook:

Size 3mm (US D, UK 10) crochet hook

Size:

3in (7.5cm) from point to point

Instructions:

Using A, make 4 ch, join into a circle with a sl st.

Round 1: 3 ch, work 11 dc (*UKtr*) into ring, join with a sl
st to top of 3 ch at beg of round. Break A.

Round 2: using B, 5 ch [counts as dc (*UKtr*) and 2 ch],
skip 1 dc (*UKtr*), *4 dc (*UKtr*) cluster in next dc (*UKtr*), 2
ch, 1 dc (*UKtr*) into next dc (*UKtr*), 2 ch*, rep from
* to * ending last rep with 2 ch, sl st to 3rd of 5 ch at
beg of round. Fasten off yarn B.

Round 3: using C, 1 sc (*UKdc*) into next 2 ch sp, 1 ch,
*[5 dc (*UKtr*), 6 ch, work 1 sl st into 3rd ch from hook
(picot made), 3 ch, 5 dc (*UKtr*)] into the top of next
cluster, 1 sc (*UKdc*) into next sp, 2 ch, 1 sc (*UKdc*) into
top of next cluster, 2 ch, 1 sc (*UKdc*) into next sp, 2 ch*,
rep from * to * twice more, sl st to beg of round. Fasten
off and work in all the ends.

To make the mat

Make 6 triangles in whatever colours you choose. Sew
them together as shown in the photograph opposite.

Edging

Join light green to any corner, work in sc (*UKdc*) evenly
all round mat [approximately 24 sc (*UKdc*) across each
motif]. Join with a sl st to beg of round. Work one more
round in light green, working 3 sc (*UKdc*) into each of
the 6 corner sts to keep the work flat. Join with a sl st
as before. Break light green. Join in dark green and
work a further round of sc (*UKdc*), working 3 sc (*UKdc*)
into the corner sts as before. Fasten off and weave in
all loose ends.

FILET FUN BEANIE

Materials:

2 balls of light worsted
(DK/8-ply) alpaca yarn
in vintage-gold yellow;
50g/109yd/100m

Stitch marker (optional)

Hooks:

Size 4mm (US G/6, UK 8)
and 5mm (US H/8, UK 6)
crochet hooks

Size:

Head circumference
21¼–22in (54–56cm)

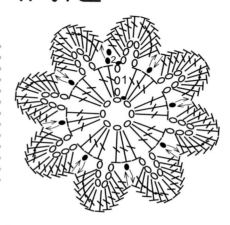

Gauge (tension) sample

5 repeats, i.e. 5 sets of 3 ch + 1 sc (UKdc), and 13
rounds in the filet pattern using the 5mm (US H/8, UK 6)
crochet hook = 3¾ x 4in (9.5 x 10cm). Change your hook
if necessary to obtain the correct gauge (tension).

Filet pattern

Work 3 ch and 1 sc (UKdc) into each 3-ch of the previous
round, working in spiral rounds. Mark the
start of the round with a contrasting yarn or crochet
stitch marker.

Instructions:

Start the beanie at the crown and work down to the
bottom edge in rounds.

To begin, 4 ch using the 5mm (US H/8, UK 6) hook and
join into a ring with a sl st. Rounds 1–2 are worked in dc
(UKtr) to produce the increases. The filet design begins
in round 3 and from round 4 onwards you will be working
into the 3-ch of the previous round.

Round 1: 3 ch (counts as 1st dc/UKtr), work 15 dc (UKtr)
into the ring then join up into a round with a sl st into the
3rd ch from the start of the round.

Round 2: 3 ch (counts as 1st dc/UKtr), 1 dc (UKtr) into
the 1st dc (UKtr) of the previous round, then work 2 dc
(UKtr) into each of the next 15 sts. Close up the round
with a sl st into the 3rd ch from the start of the round
(32 sts).

Round 3: * 3 ch, 1 sc (UKdc) * , rep from * to * into each
st of the previous round.

Round 4: From now on, work in spiral rounds in the filet-
mesh pattern, working 3 ch and 1 sc (UKdc) alternately,
and working the sc (UKdc) around the 3-ch of the
previous round.

Rounds 5–22: Rep round 4.

Round 23 (hat band): Work 1 sc (UKdc) around each
3-ch of the previous round and work 1 sc (UKdc) into
each sc (UKdc) of the previous round (64 sts).

Rounds 24–28: Change to the 4mm (US G/6, UK 8) hook
and work in spiral rounds of sc (UKdc), inserting the
hook into the horizontal back loop of each st only. Close
up the final round with a sl st.

Flower

Using the 4mm (US G/6, UK 8) hook, ch 8 and join into a
ring with a sl st.

Round 1: Work into the ring with dc (UKtr) and ch as
shown in the chart above. The numbers show the round
transitions each time. Close up the round with a sl st.
The little arrows show the direction for crocheting.

Round 2: Follow the chart, working the dc (UKtr) for
the petals around the 6-ch curves of round 1. Finish the
flower after round 2.

Making up

When you have completed the hat, attach the flower to
the band, using the photograph as a guide.

CHRISTMAS PUDDING

Instructions:

Using brown metallic yarn, make 2 ch, work 6 sc (*UKdc*) into 2nd ch from hook then join with a sl st into a ring.

Round 1: work 2 sc (*UKdc*) into each sc (*UKdc*) around, join with a sl st.

Round 2: *1 sc (*UKdc*) into next sc (*UKdc*), 2 sc (*UKdc*) into next sc (*UKdc*),* repeat from * to * all around and then join into a circle with a sl st as before.

Round 3: *1 sc (*UKdc*) into each of next 2 sc (*UKdc*), 2 sc (*UKdc*) into next sc (*UKdc*),* repeat from * to * all around and then join with sl st as before.

Round 4: *1 sc (*UKdc*) into each of next 3 sc (*UKdc*), 2 sc (*UKdc*) into next sc (*UKdc*),* repeat from * to * all around and then join with a sl st as before.

Round 5: 1 sc (*UKdc*) into each of next 4 sc (*UKdc*), 2 sc (*UKdc*) into next sc (*UKdc*),* repeat from * to * all around and then join with sl st as before.

Work 8 rounds in sc (*UKdc*) with no increase.

Now start the decreases. Stuff the pudding as you go.

Next round: *1 sc (*UKdc*) into each of next 4 sc (UKdc), sc (*UKdc*) 2 tog,* repeat from * to * all around and then join with a sl st as before.

Next round: *1 sc (*UKdc*) into each of next 3 sc (*UKdc*), sc (*UKdc*) 2 tog,* repeat from * to * all around and then join with a sl st as before.

Next round: *1 sc (*UKdc*) into each of next 2 sc (*UKdc*), sc (*UKdc*) 2 tog,* repeat from * to * all around and then join with a sl st as before.

Next round: *1 sc (*UKdc*) into next sc (*UKdc*), sc (*UKdc*) 2 tog,* repeat from * to * all around and then join as before.

Next round: sc (*UKdc*) 2 tog all around. Cut the yarn, run the end through the last row of sts, draw up and fasten off.

Iced topping

Using white crochet cotton, make 2 ch. Work 6 sc (*UKdc*) into 2nd ch from hook then join with a sl st into a ring.

Round 1: (RS) work 2 sc (*UKdc*) into each sc (*UKdc*) all around and then join with a sl st.

Materials:

1 ball of metallic yarn in brown; 25g/109yd/100m

Small amount of No. 3 crochet cotton in white; 100g/306yd/280m

20in (0.5m) of white ribbon

Holly berry embellishment

Small amount of toy stuffing

Craft glue

Hook:

Size 2mm (US B/1, UK 14) crochet hook

Size:

Approx. 2¼in (6cm) high

Round 2: *1 sc (*UKdc*) into next sc (*UKdc*), 2 sc (*UKdc*) into next sc (*UKdc*),* repeat from * to * all around and then join with a sl st as before.

Round 3: *1 sc (*UKdc*) into each of next 2 sc (*UKdc*), 2 sc (*UKdc*) into next sc (*UKdc*),* repeat from * to * all around and then join with a sl st as before.

Round 4: *1 sc (*UKdc*) into each of next 3 sc (*UKdc*), 2 sc (*UKdc*) into next sc (*UKdc*),* repeat from * to * all around and then join with a sl st as before.

Round 5: 1 sc (*UKdc*) into each of next 4 sc (*UKdc*), 2 sc (*UKdc*) into next sc (*UKdc*),* repeat from * to * all around and then join with a sl st as before.

Work 4 rounds in sc (*UKdc*) without further shaping.

Next round: working with the WS facing: *1 dc (*UKtr*) into next sc (*UKdc*), sl st into next sc (*UKdc*),* repeat from * to * all around and then join as before. Fasten off.

Making up

Weave in all loose ends. Place the iced topping over one end of the pudding and stitch in place all around. Push the holly embellishment through the centre of the icing and secure it with a few stitches or a little craft glue. Thread the ribbon through the top of the pudding to make a hanging loop and trim to length. Tie the ends of the ribbon into a knot or stitch them to form a loop.

SCABIOUS

Materials:

Small amount of multicoloured ribbon yarn

9 red bugle beads

9 small red beads

Sewing thread

Tools:

Size 4.5mm (US 7, UK 7) crochet hook

Sewing needle or beading needle

Instructions:

Make 4 ch, join with a sl st into a ring.

Round 1: *sl st into loop, 7 ch, skip 2 ch, sl st into next 5 ch*, repeat from * to * ten more times (11 petals).

Round 2: *sl st into space between petals 1 and 2 from round 1 keeping yarn behind, 6 ch, skip 2 ch, sl st into next 4 ch*, repeat from * to * ten more times, working between the petals from round 1. You should now have made 11 more petals, making 22 petals in total.

Round 3: *sl st into base ch between petals 1 and 2 from round 2, 5 ch, skip 2 ch, sl st into next 3 ch*, repeat from * to * ten more times, working between the petals. You should now have made 11 more petals, making 33 petals in total.

Round 4: sl st into base of first petal from round 3, break yarn and thread through to back of work.

Thread a needle with sewing thread and bring the thread through to the centre of the flower from the back. Thread on a bugle bead followed by a small bead, then pass the needle through the bugle bead again. Leave the thread slightly loose so that the beads are not held too tightly. Repeat for the remaining beads then secure on the back of the work with a few stitches.

Attach the flower to a ribbon to make it into a pretty bracelet, as shown in the photograph opposite.

BERNIE THE CHRISTMAS ELF

Materials:

1 ball each of No. 5 crochet cotton in beige and red, and small amounts in dark brown and mid-green; 100g/437yd/400m

Black floss for embroidering features

3 tiny gold beads for hat

Toy stuffing

Sewing threads to match crochet cotton

Tools:

Size 2.5mm (US B/1, UK 13) crochet hook

Sewing needle

Instructions:

Make the bear following the instructions on page 37, using beige for the head, body, arms and legs and dark brown for the muzzle and ears.

Sleeves

Row 1: using red, make 17 ch, 1 dc (UKtr) in 3rd ch from hook, 1 dc (UKtr) in each ch to end, turn.

Rows 2–4: 3 ch, skip 1 st, 1 dc (UKtr) in each st to end.

Row 5: 1 ch, 1 sc (UKdc) in each st to end. Fasten off.

Tunic (make 2)

Row 1: using red, make 20 ch, dc (UKtr) in 3rd ch from hook, 1 dc (UKtr) in each ch to end, turn.

Rows 2 and 3: 3 ch, skip 1 st, 1 dc (UKtr) in each dc (UKtr) to end.

Row 4: 3 ch, skip 1 st, dc (UKtr) 2 tog, dc (UKtr) to last 3 sts, dc (UKtr) 2 tog, 1 dc (UKtr) in last st.

Row 5: sl st across next 4 dc (UKtr), 3 ch, 1 dc (UKtr) in each dc (UKtr) to last 3 dc (UKtr), turn.

Row 6: 3 ch, dc (UKtr) in each st to end.

Row 7: 3 ch, 1 dc (UKtr), 1 hdc (UKhtr), 5 sc (UKdc), 1 hdc (UKhtr), 2 dc (UKtr). Fasten off.

Collar

Using green, make 24 ch, 1 sc (UKdc) in 2nd ch from hook, dc (UKtr) 2 tog over next 2 ch. Fasten off.

Rejoin yarn to next ch, 3ch, dc (UKtr) 2 tog over next 2 ch. Fasten off. Rep from * to * along rest of ch, ending 1 sc (UKdc) in last ch.

Hat

Row 1: using green, make 26 ch, 1 sc (UKdc) in 2nd ch from hook, 1 sc (UKdc) in each ch to end, turn.

Row 2: 1 ch, 1 sc (UKdc) in each st to end, turn.

Rows 3 and 4: changing to red, 3 ch, skip 1 st, 1 dc (UKtr) in each st to end, turn.

Rows 5 and 6: 3 ch, skip 1 st, dc (UKtr) 2 tog across row to last st, 1 dc (UKtr) in last st, turn.

Rows 7 and 8: 3 ch, 1 dc (UKtr) in each st to end.

Row 9: 3 ch, dc (UKtr) 2 tog three times, 1 dc (UKtr) in last tr, turn.

Row 10: 3 ch, skip 1 dc (UKtr), 1 dc (UKtr) in each st to end. Break yarn.

Run thread through last row, draw up and secure.

Belt

Using green, make ch long enough to go round the bear's waist with a little extra for overlap. Fasten off.

Making up

Work in the ends on all the pieces. Catch the back and front tunic pieces at the shoulder edges to hold them in place. Stitch the sleeves in place. Sew the side and sleeve seams and put the tunic on to the bear. Sew the shoulder seams on either side. Sew the seam on the hat and attach three tiny gold beads to the point. Place the belt around the bear's waist and catch the ends together at the centre back. Place the collar around the bear's neck and join at the centre back. Stretch it slightly to give a good fit.

LUCY PURSE

Materials:
1 ball each of lace weight (2-ply) yarn in light
   brown (A), brown (B), yellow (C) and green (D);
   25g/229yd/210m

Hook:
4mm (US G/6, UK 8) crochet hook

Notions:
1 x purse clasp approx. 9in (23cm) wide

Size:
Approx. 11¾in (30cm) at the widest point and
   6in (15cm) high

Special abbreviation

Front post sc (fpsc) – *UKfpdc*: insert hook from the
front to the back around the post of the sc (*UKdc*) on the
previous row. Complete as for regular sc (*UKdc*).

Instructions (make 2):

Work in pattern following the stripe sequence as follows:
Rows 7 and 8: yarn A; Rows 9 and 10: yarn B; Rows 11
and 12: yarn C; Rows 13 and 14: yarn D.

With yarn A and 4mm (US G/6, UK 8) crochet hook,
make 45 ch.

Row 1: 1 sc (*UKdc*) into second ch from hook, 1 sc
(*UKdc*) in every ch to end (44 sts).

Row 2: 1 ch, 1 sc (*UKdc*) in every st to end.

Rep row 2 four more times.

Row 7: 3 ch (counts as 1 dc (*UKtr*)), 1 dc (*UKtr*) in next
4 sts, *[5 dc (*UKtr*) in next st] twice, 1 dc (*UKtr*) in next
6 sts, rep from * three times, [5 dc (*UKtr*) in next st]
twice, 1 dc (*UKtr*) in next 5 sts.

Row 8: 1 ch, 1 fpsc (*UKfpdc*) in each st to end.

Row 9: Change to colour B, 3 ch (counts as 1 dc (*UKtr*)),
working in tops of fpsc (*UKfpdc*) row, [1 dc (*UKtr*) in next
st, skip next st] four times, [5 dc (*UKtr*) in next st] twice,
*skip 2 sts, [1 dc (*UKtr*) in next st, skip 1 st] twice, 1 dc
(*UKtr*) in next st, [1 dc (*UKtr*) in next st, skip 1 st] twice,
1 dc (*UKtr*) in next st, skip 2 sts, [5 dc (*UKtr*) in next
st] twice, rep from * three more times, skip 1 st, [1 dc
(*UKtr*) in next st, skip 1 st] three times, 1 dc (*UKtr*) in
each of last 2 sts.

Row 10: As row 8.

Rows 9 and 10 form the pattern, rep the pattern twice
more, following the colour sequence.

Row 15: Change to colour A, 3 ch (counts as 1 dc
(*UKtr*)), working in tops of fpsc (*UKfpdc*) row, 2 dc (*UKtr*)
in st at base of ch, [1 dc (*UKtr*) in next st, skip next st]
four times, [5 dc (*UKtr*) in next st] twice, *skip 2 sts, [1
dc (*UKtr*) in next st, skip 1 st] twice, 1 dc (*UKtr*) in next
st, [1 dc (*UKtr*) in next st, skip 1 st] twice, 1 dc (*UKtr*) in
next st, skip 2 sts, [5 dc (*UKtr*) in next st] twice, rep from
* three more times, skip 1 st, [1 dc (*UKtr*) in next st, skip
1 st] three times, 1 dc (*UKtr*) in next st, 3 dc (*UKtr*) in
last st (48 sts).

Row 16: As row 8.

Row 17: Change to colour B, 3 ch (counts as 1 dc
(*UKtr*)), working in tops of fpsc (*UKfpdc*) row, 1 dc (*UKtr*)
in st at base of ch, [1 dc (*UKtr*) in next st, skip next st]
five times, [5 dc (*UKtr*) in next st] twice, *skip
2 sts, [1 dc (*UKtr*) in next st, skip 1 st] twice, 1 dc (*UKtr*)
in next st, [1 dc (*UKtr*) in next st, skip 1 st] twice, 1 dc
(*UKtr*) in next st, skip 2 sts, [5 dc (*UKtr*) in next st] twice,
rep from * three more times, skip 1 st, [1 dc (*UKtr*) in
next st, skip 1 st] four times, 1 dc (*UKtr*) in next st, 2 dc
(*UKtr*) in last st.

Row 18: As row 8.

Rows 17 to 18 form the pattern; rep the pattern six more
times, following the colour sequence as set, ending last
row on row 18 of pattern in colour D.

Fasten off yarn.

Making up

Do not press. Weave in all loose ends. Using mattress
stitch and with RS together, join the back and front
pieces along the lower edge and 3¼in (8cm) up both
sides. Turn through, line the purse if desired, then attach
the clasp.

PICOT HEXAGON

Materials:
Small amounts of No. 3 crochet cotton
in pink (A), cerise (B), purple (C) and
green (D); 100g/306yd/280m

Hook:
Size 3mm (US D, UK 10) crochet hook

Size:
Approx. 3½in (9cm) across

Instructions:

Using A, make 6 ch, join into a ring with a sl st.

Round 1: work 1 ch, 12 sc (*UKdc*) into ring, join to 1st ch with a sl st.

Round 2: work 1 ch, 2 sc (*UKdc*) into each sc (*UKdc*) to end. Break A.

Round 3: using B, work 3 ch, 3 dc (*UKtr*) into same ch as join, *4 ch, skip 3 sc (*UKdc*), 4 dc (*UKtr*) into next sc (*UKdc*)*, rep from * to * all round, ending with 4 ch, join to top of 3 ch at beg of round [6 x 4 dc (*UKtr*) groups]. Break B.

Round 4: using C, work 3 ch, 1 dc (*UKtr*) into each of next 3 dc (*UKtr*), but leaving last loop of each st on hook, yrh, draw loop through all loops on hook, *5 ch, 1 sc (*UKdc*) into 4 ch loop, 5 ch**, 1 dc (*UKtr*) into each of next 4 dc (*UKtr*), leaving last loop of each dc (*UKtr*) on hook, yrh, draw loop through all loops on

hook*. Rep from * to * all round but ending last rep at **. Join with a sl st to top of 4 dc (*UKtr*) group at beg of round. Break C.

Round 5: using D, in same place as sl st make 3 ch, work a sl st into 4th ch from hook (picot made), *4 sc (*UKdc*) into next 5 ch loop, 1 sc (*UKdc*) into next sc (*UKdc*), 4 sc (*UKdc*) into next 5 ch loop**, 1 sc (*UKdc*) into top of group, 3 ch, sl st into 3rd ch from hook (picot made)*, rep from * to * all round, ending last rep at **, sl st to top of first group, fasten off. Weave in all loose ends.

SHADES OF GREY HAT

Materials:

2 balls of super bulky (super chunky) wool/mohair blend self-striping yarn in anthracite; 50g/54yd/50m

Tools:

Size 8mm (US L/11) and 15mm (US Q) crochet hooks

Pompom maker set (optional)

Size:

Head circumference 21¼–23in (54–58cm)

Gauge (tension) sample

8 sts, i.e. 1 bobble + 1 ch alternately four times, and 6.5 rounds in the basic pattern using the 15mm (US Q) crochet hook = 4 x 4in (10 x 10cm). Change your hook if necessary to obtain the correct gauge (tension).

Basic pattern

Round 1: 1 ch, pick up 1 loop each from the 1st and 2nd sc (*UKdc*) of the previous round. Pull this as high as possible, yrh, draw the yarn through all 3 loops on the hook together to make a bobble. Now 1 ch, pick up 1 loop from the 2nd sc (*UKdc*) and then from the 3rd sc (*UKdc*) of the previous round, yrh, then draw the yarn through all 3 loops on the hook together to make the 2nd bobble. Continue working in this way until you have made 16 bobbles, each followed by 1 ch.

Round 2 onwards: 1 ch, pick up 1 loop each under the 1st and 2nd ch of the previous round, pull this fairly high, yrh, draw the yarn through all 3 loops on the hook together to make a bobble. Now 1 ch, pick up another loop each under the 2nd and 3rd ch of the previous round, yrh, draw the yarn through all 3 sts on the hook together to make the 2nd bobble. 1 ch and continue working in the same way in spiral rounds, alternating 1 bobble and 1 ch each time.

Instructions:

Start the beanie at the top and work down to the bottom edge in spiral rounds.

Begin with 2 ch using the 15mm (US P/16) hook.

Round 1: Work 8 sc (*UKdc*) into the 2nd ch from the hook (see page 20).

Round 2: Work 2 sc (*UKdc*) into each st around (16 sts).

Rounds 3–16: Work in the basic pattern following the instructions above.

Hat band

When the piece is roughly 9¾in (25cm) long, change to the 8mm (US L/11, UK 0) hook and work 2 sc (*UKdc*) into each st around (32 sts). Work another spiral round of sc (*UKdc*) without increase. When the piece is roughly 10½in (27cm) long, close the round with a sl st.

Making up

Using leftover yarn, make a pompom about 2¾in (7cm) in diameter. Use a pompom maker or cut cardboard rings to work over (see page 18). Sew the pompom to the top of the hat.

TABLETOP TREE

Materials:

1 ball each of No. 3 crochet
   cotton in green and
   variegated green;
   100g/306yd/280m
Scrap of mini tinsel

Mini coloured tinsel balls
2 gold stars
Cocktail stick
Craft glue
Small amount of stuffing

Hook:

Size 2mm (US B/1, UK 14)
   crochet hook

Size:

Approx. 3¼in (8cm) high

Instructions:

Tree

Using green crochet cotton, make 40 ch and join with a sl st into a circle, being careful not to twist the chain.

Round 1: work 1 sc (*UKdc*) into each ch around then join with a sl st to beg of round (40 sts).

Work a further 3 rounds of sc (*UKdc*).

Round 5: *1 sc (*UKdc*) into each of next 3 sc (*UKdc*), sc (*UKdc*) 2 tog,* repeat from * to * all around (32 sts).

Work 4 rounds in sc (*UKdc*).

Next round: *1 sc (*UKdc*) into each of next 2 sc (*UKdc*), sc (*UKdc*) 2 tog,* repeat from * to * all around (24 sts).

Work 4 rounds in sc (*UKdc*).

Next round: *1 sc (*UKdc*) into next sc (*UKdc*), sc (*UKdc*) 2 tog,* repeat from * to * all around (16 sts).

Work 4 rounds in sc (*UKdc*).

Next round: sc (*UKdc*) 2 tog all around (8 sts).

Work 2 rounds in sc (*UKdc*).

Next round: sc (*UKdc*) 2 tog all around. Fasten off.

Base

Using green yarn, make 2 ch.

Round 1: work 6 sc (*UKdc*) into 2nd ch from hook then join with a sl st into a tight circle.

Round 2: 2 sc (*UKdc*) into each st around then join with a sl st to beg (12 sts).

Round 3: *1 sc (*UKdc*) into next sc (*UKdc*), 2 sc (*UKdc*) into next sc (*UKdc*),* repeat from * to * all around then join with a sl st as before (18 sts).

Round 4: *1 sc (*UKdc*) into each of next 2 sc (*UKdc*), 2 sc (*UKdc*) into next sc (*UKdc*),* repeat from * to * all around then join with a sl st (24 sts).

Round 5: * 1 sc (*UKdc*) into each of next 3 sc (*UKdc*), 2 sc (*UKdc*) into next sc (*UKdc*),* repeat from * to * all around then join with a sl st (30 sts).

Round 6: 1 sc (*UKdc*) into each of next 4 sc (*UKdc*), 2 sc (*UKdc*) into next sc (*UKdc*),* repeat from * to * all around then join with a sl st (36 sts).

Round 7: 1 sc (*UKdc*) into each of next 5 sc (*UKdc*), 2 sc (*UKdc*) into next sc (*UKdc*),* repeat from * to * all around then join with a sl st (42 sts). Fasten off.

Twisted strands (make 1 in each of 4 sizes)

Using variegated green crochet cotton, make 20 ch. Work 1 dc (*UKtr*) into 3rd ch from hook, then 3 dc (*UKtr*) into each ch to end. The crochet will twist as you work. Fasten off. Repeat the process starting with 28 ch, 30 ch and 36 ch.

Making up

Work in all the ends. Stuff the tree quite firmly then attach the base, inverting it slightly to enable the tree to stand. Take each twisted strand and sew the ends together to form a circle. Place the circles on the tree in size order, starting with the largest at the base. Sew in place.

Wrap some tinsel around the tree, securing it with a little craft glue or stitches. Glue the tinsel balls on to the branches at random. Cut the cocktail stick in half. Place a little glue on one side of a star and press the other star on to it, sandwiching half the cocktail stick in between. Press firmly until well stuck. Push the cocktail stick down into the top of the tree, securing it with a little glue.

ORANGE BLOSSOM

Materials:

- Small amounts of No. 3 crochet cotton in yellow and white; 100g/306yd/280m
- Various small orange beads
- Orange sewing thread

Tools:

- Size 2.5mm (US B/1, UK 13) crochet hook
- Sewing needle

Instructions:

Using yellow crochet cotton, make 4 ch, join with a sl st into a ring (see page 20).

Round 1: 1 ch, 5 sc (*UKdc*) into ring, sl st into 1 ch.

Round 2: 2 ch, 1 dc (*UKtr*) into each sc (*UKdc*), sl st to join, tie off the end.

Rejoin white crochet cotton at base of work, work into sc (*UKdc*) strand.

Round 3: *6 ch, skip 1 ch, 1 sc (*UKdc*) into next ch, 1 hdc (*UKhtr*) into next ch, 1 dc (*UKtr*) into next ch, 1 tr (*UKdtr*) into next ch, 1 dtr (*UKttr*) into next ch, sl st into next st of

first round*, repeat from * to * four more times, making 5 petals in total. End in same st as join.

Tie off and sew in the ends.

Join the sewing thread to the reverse of the flower and push the needle up through the space between the yellow centre and the white ridge surrounding it. Thread on a bead and take the thread back through to the back of the work. Repeat, sewing on beads all around the yellow flower centre.

These pretty little flowers look great on accessories around the home – try them on hanging hearts, napkin rings, jewellery boxes and notebooks, for example, to add that personal touch.

MARY PARTY BEAR

Materials:

- 1 ball each of No. 5 crochet cotton in ecru and red; 100g/437yd/400m
- Small amount of crochet cotton in very light beige
- Brown floss for embroidering features
- Short strip of red sequins
- Small piece of marabou in bright red
- String of approx. 50 small pearl beads
- Toy stuffing
- Sewing threads to match crochet cotton

Tools:

- Size 2.5mm (US B/1, UK 13) crochet hook
- Sewing needle

Instructions:

Make the bear following the instructions on page 37, using ecru for the head, body, arms and legs and very light beige for the muzzle and ears.

Dress back

Row 1: Using red crochet cotton, make 21 ch, 1 sc (UKdc) in 2nd ch from hook, 1 sc (UKdc) in each ch to end, turn (20 sts).

Row 2: 1 ch, 1 sc (UKdc) in each sc (UKdc) to end, turn.

Row 3: rep row 2.

Row 4: sc (UKdc) 2 tog at each end of row (18 sts).

Row 5: sc (UKdc) to end.

Rows 6 and 7: rep rows 4 and 5 (16 sts).

Rows 8–10: sc (UKdc) to end.

Row 11: sl st across 3 sc (UKdc), work until 3 sc (UKdc) rem, turn.*

Work on these 10 sts for a further 8 rows. Fasten off.

Make frill along bottom edge of dress by working 2 dc (UKtr) in each st all along the starting chain. Fasten off.

Dress front

Work as dress back to *.

Continue on these sts for a further 4 rows.

Next row: work across 2 sc (UKdc), turn.

Continue on these 2 sts until strap matches back to shoulder. Fasten off.

Skip centre 6 sc (UKdc), join in yarn and complete to match other strap.

Work frill along bottom edge as for dress back.

Making up

Work the bear's features in brown floss. Sew the side seams of the dress. Take the sequin strip and measure enough to go all round the bottom of the dress. Stitch it in place along the last row of sc (UKdc), sewing through the centre of each sequin. Slip the dress on to the bear and sew the shoulder seams. Place the string of pearls around the bear's neck and tie it off firmly at the centre back of the neck. To make the headdress, wrap a piece of sequin strip around the bear's head, overlap it slightly at the back and stitch the two ends together. Take a tiny piece of marabou and stitch it to the join. Position the headdress on the bear's head and sew it in place with a few stitches. Cut a short length of the marabou to make a feather boa and drape it around the bear's neck.

ISABEL PURSE

Materials:

1 ball of worsted (light aran) yarn in lilac (A); 100g/219yd/200m

1 ball of lace weight (2-ply) yarn in light pink (B); 25g/229yd/210m

Oddments of worsted yarn (light aran) in green (C)

Hook:

4mm (US G/6, UK 8) crochet hook

Notions:

1 x purse clasp approx. 3½in (9cm) wide

Approx. 102 x small beads

Size:

Approx. 3¾ x 4¼in (9.5 x 10.75cm)

Instructions:

Make 2 purse motifs

With yarn A and 4mm (US G/6, UK 8) crochet hook, make 4 ch and join with sl st to form a ring.

Round 1: 1 ch, 8 sc (UKdc) into ring, sl st to first sc (UKdc) (8 sts).

Round 2: 1 ch, work 2 sc (UKdc) into every sc (UKdc), sl st to first sc (UKdc) (16 sts).

Round 3: 1 ch, *1 sc (UKdc) into next sc (UKdc), 2 sc (UKdc) into next sc (UKdc), rep from * to end, sl st to first sc (UKdc) (24 sts).

Round 4: 1 ch, * 1 sc (UKdc) into each of next 2 sc (UKdc), 2 sc (UKdc) into next sc (UKdc), rep from * to end, sl st to first sc (UKdc) (32 sts).

Round 5: 1 ch, * 1 sc (UKdc) into next 3 sc (UKdc), 2 sc (UKdc) into next sc (UKdc), rep from * to end, sl st to first sc (UKdc) (40 sts).

Rounds 6 and 7: 1 ch, 1 sc (UKdc) into every sc (UKdc) to end, sl st to first sc (UKdc), turn after round 7.

Row 8: 1 ch, 1 sc (UKdc) into base of ch, 1 sc (UKdc) into next 22 sc (UKdc), turn.

Rows 9 and 10: 1 ch, 1 sc (UKdc) into base of ch, 1 sc (UKdc) into next 22 sc (UKdc), 1 sc (UKdc) into ch made on previous round, turn.

Fasten off yarn.

Rose

Thread 102 beads onto yarn B.

With 4mm (US G/6, UK 8) crochet hook and yarn B, make 57 ch.

Row 1: (dc (UKtr), ch 2, dc (UKtr)) in sixth ch from hook (5 skipped chs count as first dc (UKtr) plus 2 ch), *ch 2, skip next 2 chs, (dc (UKtr), ch 2, dc (UKtr)) in next ch; rep from * across (36 sps).

Row 2: 3 ch (counts as first dc (UKtr)), working one bead into each dc (UKtr) continue as follows: 5 dc (UKtr) in next 2-ch sp, sc (UKdc) in next 2-ch sp, *6 dc (UKtr) in next 2-ch sp, sc (UKdc) in next 2-ch sp, rep from * to end.

Fasten off leaving a long piece of yarn for sewing the rose together.

With RS facing and beg with last petal made, roll petals to form rose; sew to secure as you roll with the length of yarn left.

Leaf (make 2)

With 4mm (US G/6, UK 8) crochet hook and yarn C, make 10 ch.

Round 1: 1 sc (UKdc) into second ch from hook, 1 hdc (UKhtr) in next ch, 1 dc (UKtr) in next ch, 1 tr (UKdtr) in next 3 ch, 1 dc (UKtr) in next 3 ch, 1 hdc (UKhtr) in next ch, 1 sc (UKdc) in next ch.

Fasten off yarn.

Making up

With WS together, join the two larger sides of the purse together with a row of sc (UKdc). Attach the purse clasp and sew the rose and leaves to the front of the purse. Attach a lining if desired.

AUTUMN SQUARE

Materials:
Small amounts of No. 3 crochet cotton
    in peach (A), yellow (B) and brown (C);
    100g/306yd/280m

Hook:
Size 3mm (US D, UK 10)
    crochet hook

Size:
3in (7.5cm) diameter

Instructions:

Using A, make 4 ch and join into a circle with
a sl st.

Round 1: 5 ch [counts as 1 dc (UKtr) and 2
ch], *1 dc (UKtr), 2 ch into ring*, rep from *
to * eleven times, join to 3 ch at beg of round.
Fasten off yarn A.

Round 2: using B, 3 ch, 2 dc (UKtr), leaving
last loop of each st on hook, yrh and draw
through all loops [3 dc (UKtr) cluster made],
3 ch, 3 dc (UKtr) cluster into 2 ch sp, rep
from * to * all round, ending last rep with 2
ch, sl st to top of 3 ch at beg of round.
Fasten off yarn B.

Round 3: using C, sl st into first 2 ch sp, *1
sc (UKdc) into sp, 4 ch*, rep from * to * all
round, sl st into sc (UKdc) at beg of round.

Round 4: *5 dc (UKtr), 3 ch, 5 dc (UKtr) into
next 4 ch sp, 1 sc (UKdc) into next 4 ch sp, 3
ch, 1 sc (UKdc) into next 4 ch sp*, rep from
* to * three more times, sl st to dc (UKtr) at
beg of round. Fasten off and weave in all
loose ends.

STREET SMART BEANIE

Materials:

1 ball each of aran tweed yarn in silver grey, raspberry, lavender and plum; 50g/126yd/115m

Hooks:

Sizes 4.5mm (US 7, UK 7) and 6mm (US J/10, UK 4) crochet hooks

Size:

Head circumference 21¼–23in (54–58cm)

Gauge (tension) sample:

Rounds 1–2 of the crochet pattern using the 4.5mm (US 7, UK 7) hook = 3¾in (9.5cm) diameter and rounds 1–5 = 7in (18cm).

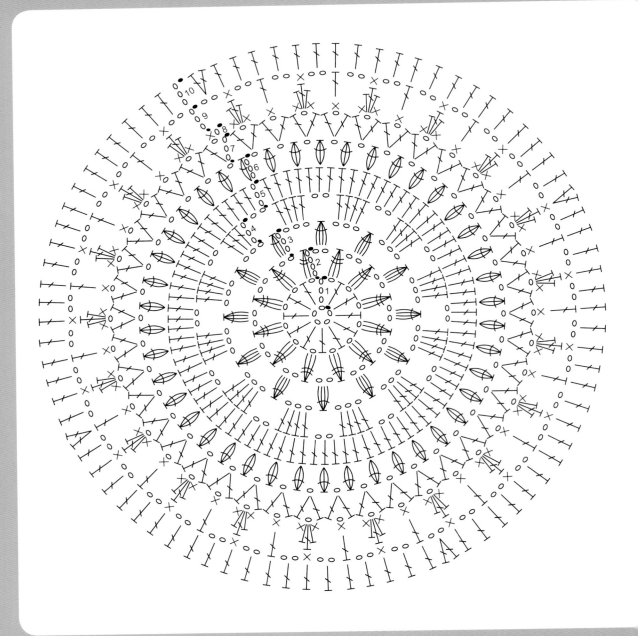

Basic pattern

The chart for the pattern is shown opposite. Work rounds 1–10 following the chart and using the colours listed in 'Changing colours' below. The rounds are shown in full. Start the round with 1, 3 or 4 ch and end with a sl st into the 1st, 3rd or 4th ch of the start of the round respectively. The foundation ch of a round is made up each time of 1 dc (*UKtr*) and 1 tr (*UKdtr*) and 1 sc (*UKdc*) respectively. The numbers show the round transitions each time. Always crochet the dctog (*UKtrtog*) and trtog (*UKdtrtog*) around the ch of the previous round. For each puff, work dc3tog (*UKtr3tog*) in the same st.

Changing colours

Work 1 round each in silver, raspberry, lavender and plum. Repeat this sequence once more. Work rounds 9 and 10 in silver grey and then work rounds 11–18 as explained below. When changing colour, the new colour should be introduced on the last loop of the st just before the st that will be made in the new colour to give a perfect colour transition.

Tip

If the new colour begins with a few sts before the start of the next round, always continue crocheting with 1 sl st in the new colour at the appropriate place.

Instructions:

Start the beanie at the crown and work down to the bottom edge.

Using the 4.5mm (US 7, UK 7) crochet hook and silver-grey yarn, begin with 5 ch and join into a ring with a sl st (see page 20).

Rounds 1–10: Work following the chart (see opposite) and 'Changing colours' (left), working the first round into the ring. After round 10 there will be 88 sts. Now work as follows, closing up each round with a sl st:

Round 11 (raspberry): Work as for round 6, including the start of round by alternately working 1 puff into each 2nd dc (*UKtr*) of the previous round and then 1 ch.

Round 12 (lavender): 3 ch (= 1 dc/*UKtr*), work 1 dc (*UKtr*) around 1 ch of the previous round * , work 2 dc (*UKtr*) around the following ch of the previous round * , rep from * to * around.

Round 13 (plum): 3 ch (= 1 dc/*UKtr*), work dc2tog (*UKtr2tog*) all around (44 sts).

Round 14 (silver grey): 3 ch (= 1 dc/UKtr), dc (*UKtr*) into each st around (44 sts).

Round 15 (raspberry): 2 ch (= 1 hdc/*UKhtr*), hdc (*UKhtr*) into each st around.

Rounds 16–18 (lavender band): For the edge, change to the 6mm (US J/10, UK 4) hook and work another 3 rounds of sc (*UKdc*), starting each round with 1 ch and closing up with a sl st. Fasten off and weave in all loose ends.

POINSETTIA GIFT TOPPER

Materials:

1 ball each of metallic yarn in red, green and gold; 25g/109yd/100m

35½in (90cm) of red gold-edged satin ribbon, 1in (2.5cm) wide

Gold flower bead stamens

Fine florist's wire or rose wire

Red sewing thread

Tools:

Size 2mm (US B-1, UK 14) crochet hook

Sewing needle

Size:

Approx. 2¼in (6cm) in diameter

Instructions:

Flower 1 (6 petals)

Using red yarn, make 6 ch then join with sl st into a ring.

Round 1: 1 ch, work 12 sc (*UKdc*) into the ring, join with a sl st to first ch.

Round 2: *5 ch, skip 1 sc (*UKdc*), 1 sc (*UKdc*) into next sc (*UKdc*),* repeat from * to * all around, join to 1st of 5 ch at beg of round (6 x 5-ch loops).

Round 3: sl st into first 5-ch loop, 2 ch, work 5 dc (*UKtr*) into same loop, 1 sc (*UKdc*) in next sc (*UKdc*), *6 dc (*UKtr*) into 5 ch loop, 1 sc (*UKdc*) into next sc (*UKdc*),* repeat from * to * four times more, join with a sl st to beg of round.

Round 4: sl st to 2nd dc (*UKtr*), 2 ch, 1 dc (*UKtr*) into same dc (*UKtr*), 2 dc (*UKtr*) into each of next 3 dc (*UKtr*),

1 sc (*UKdc*) into next sc (*UKdc*),* skip next dc (*UKtr*), 2 dc (*UKtr*) into each of next 4 dc (*UKtr*), skip 1 dc (*UKtr*), 1 sc (*UKdc*) into sc (*UKdc*),* repeat from * to * four times more and then join with a sl st to beg of round. Break off red.

Round 5: join in gold to same place as sl st and work *1 sc (*UKdc*) into each of the next 4 dc (*UKtr*), 3 ch, sl st into 1st of the these ch (1 picot formed), 1 sc (*UKdc*) into each of the next 4 dc (*UKtr*), 1 sc (*UKdc*) into corresponding sc (*UKdc*) of row 3, thus pulling up a long loop,* repeat from * to * five times more, join with a sl st to beg of round.

Fasten off.

Flower 2 (8 petals)

Using red yarn, make 8 ch then join with a sl st into a ring.

Round 1: 1 ch, work 16 sc (*UKdc*) into the ring, join with a sl st to first ch.

Round 2: 1 ch, sc (*UKdc*) into same st as join, *1 ch, skip next sc (*UKdc*), sc (*UKdc*) into next sc (*UKdc*), 8 ch, sc (*UKdc*) into same st,* rep from * to * six times more, 1 ch, skip 1 sc (*UKdc*), sc (*UKdc*) into same st as first sc (*UKdc*), (4 ch, tr [*UKdtr*]) into same st (8 loops made).

Round 3: 3 ch to count as first dc (*UKtr*), work 7 more dc (*UKtr*) into same loop (working around the 4 ch of round 2), 1 sc (*UKdc*) into next 1 ch sp, *15 dc (*UKtr*) into next 8 ch loop, 1 sc (*UKdc*) in next 1ch sp,* repeat from * to * six more times, 7 dc (*UKtr*) into the first loop, join with a sl st to the top of beg 3 ch (8 petals made). Fasten off red yarn.

Round 4: join in gold with a sl st to beg of previous round, work 1 sc (*UKdc*) into each dc (*UKtr*) all around each petal, join with a sl st to beg of round. Fasten off.

Leaves (make 3)

Using green yarn, make 13 ch.

Work 1 sc (*UKdc*) into 2nd ch from hook, 1 hdc (*UKhtr*) into each of next 2 ch, 1 dc (*UKtr*) into each of next 2 ch, 1 tr (*UKdtr*) into each of next 2 ch, 1 dc (*UKtr*) into each of next 2 ch, 1 hdc (*UKhtr*) into next 2 ch, 1 sc (*UKdc*) into last ch. Make 1 ch, now work along the other side of the foundation in the same way, join with a sl st.

Making up

Work in the ends neatly on all the pieces. Take a wire stamen and spread the beads into a flat shape. Insert it through the centre of a flower, twist the wire into a neat coil at the back of the flower and secure with some firm stitches using a needle and red thread. Repeat with the other flower.

To make a bow

Cut the red ribbon into three 12in (30cm) lengths. Find the points 3in (7.5cm) from each end of the first length. Pinch the ribbon at these points and bring the pinches together. Squash the ribbon loop between the pinched folds so it is flat and centred at the folds. Repeat with the other ribbon lengths. When you are satisfied with the result, assemble the bows then take some fine wire and twist it tightly around the centre. Arrange the loops and tails of the ribbon in a pleasing manner then trim the tails if desired. Arrange the flowers and leaves on to the centre of the ribbon, pin in position and then sew in place.

PUBLISHER'S NOTE
If you would like more information about crochet, try
Crochet for the Absolute Beginner
by Pauline Turner, Search Press, 2014.

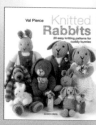

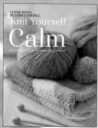